A Renewed Spirituality

Finding

Fresh

Paths

at Midlife

Lynne M. Baab

InterVarsity Press
Downers Grove, Illinois

InterVarsity Press
P.O. Box 1400, Downers Grove, IL 60515-1426
World Wide Web: www.ivpress.com
E-mail: mail@ivpress.com

InterVarsity Press® is the book-publishing division of InterVarsity Christian Fellowship/USA®, a student movement active on campus at hundreds of universities, colleges and schools of nursing in the United States of America, and a member movement of the International Fellowship of Evangelical Students. For information about local and regional activities, write Public Relations Dept., InterVarsity Christian Fellowship/USA, 6400 Schroeder Rd., P.O. Box 7895, Madison, WI 53707-7895, or visit the IVCF website at <www.ivcf.org>.

Cover photograph: Dale Sanders/Masterfile
ISBN 0-8308-2344-1
Printed in the United States of America ∞

Library of Congress Cataloging-in-Publication Data

Baab, Lynne M.
  A renewed spirituality : finding fresh paths at midlife / Lynne M. Baab.
    p. cm.
  ISBN 0-8308-2344-1 (pbk.: alk. paper)
    1. Middle aged persons—Religious life. I. Title.
  BV4579.5 B33 2002
  248.8'4—dc21

                                                                    2001059394

P	18	17	16	15	14	13	12	11	10	9	8	7	6	5	4	3	2	1
Y	16	15	14	13	12	11	10	09	08	07	06	05	04	03	02			

Contents

161

120878

Foreword

My first encounter with the author of this book was in her collegiate days in the 1970s at Willamette University in Salem, Oregon. I had just become a staff worker with InterVarsity Christian Fellowship in the Pacific Northwest, where Lynne was one of the Christian student leaders. My very first day on the Willamette campus I met Lynne: curious, bright, serious about God, honest, sensitive to others, fun and intense at the same time, and a big picture thinker.

What struck me so powerfully about Lynne as a student still impresses me today. Above all, Lynne has a heart for God. But I use that phrase not in the sentimental sense that is commonly understood today. Lynne has a passion to know God, a passion to understand what it means to be human, and a passion to understand how the two connect. She is a person who wants to understand intuitively the human landscape from the inside out, and systematically the complex range of human experience from the outside in.

This book tackles the subject of midlife: the common themes, losses and discoveries that often accompany the midlife journey. That analysis alone I found very helpful as Lynne put expression and definition to many of my own present midlife questions and experiences.

Because Lynne reads widely and thinks clearly, she is also able to expose the reader to a variety of rich spiritual traditions and disciplines that she believes—rightly so—will be enriching and deepening to the midlife pilgrim. She explores the significance of the importance of Sabbath-keeping, embracing mystery, contemplative prayer, and Celtic and Benedictine spiritualities. As I have been journeying through midlife, I have found great comfort in these ways of stepping back from the frantic pressures each day brings.

I believe this book will be of great benefit to any Christian, midlife or otherwise, who feels stuck, and who longs to draw closer to God and to feel the fresh touch of God's grace.

Rebecca Manley Pippert

Preface

In many ways this book emerged from dozens of conversations, spread over a decade, with people between 35 and 55. Sometimes I imagine sitting in a giant room full of all the people who talked to me about their experiences at midlife. In my imaginary room, fascinating conversations about this life stage swirl around me. One person talks about the loss of her parents, and another builds on her comments, mentioning the huge transition and sense of emptiness he experienced when his kids entered their teens and then left home. One man describes his deepening prayer life, and another person recounts the freedom she feels now that she has received more healing from God for childhood abuse.

I have been deeply privileged to listen to a wealth of stories about the great challenges and rich growth that happen in the midlife years. Sometimes I feel frustrated that our culture and our churches do so little to validate this stage in life. Children, youth, young adults and seniors are all served by specialized programs and ministries, and we are aware of their unique needs. But midlife is also a rich stage in the life cycle, with developmental tasks to be accomplished and significant growth to be embraced.

We often think that the middle years of adulthood are like a level plain after the tumult and exciting discoveries of early adulthood and before the adjustments and decline of retirement and old age. Instead, in the stories I listened to, I heard a variety of intense emotions in response to unanticipated losses and surprising new discoveries. I heard about intense reflection on the meaning of life. I heard about finding God in new and unexpected places. In most people's experience, midlife is far from a static, placid stage of life.

Fundamental to our Christian identity is a call to growth. If we are followers of Christ, we are being transformed into his likeness from "one degree of glory to another" (1 Cor 3:18). We are disciples of a master teacher who is calling us to learn and grow and change. We can expect that God will use all the ups and downs of every stage of our lives in his work of transforming us. This transformation will change us inwardly as we grow in drawing near to God. We will also be shaped in new ways for service and ministry; our renewed love for God will flow into renewed love and care for the people around us.

My own midlife journey began a decade ago when I was in my late thirties. After ten years of mothering two children and attending seminary part time, I finished my Master of Divinity degree. My sons were approaching their teen years, and I could see their growing independence and their decreasing need of my constant attention. I knew I wanted to find meaningful work by the time they entered adolescence.

I found myself full of questions. What could I offer the world? For what purpose had God designed me? What did I want from life? What did I value, desire and care about? Who was I, and why was I here?

All my questions did not add up to anything close to a midlife crisis. The questioning did, however, mark a transition. I knew my life would change as I moved into the working world. I would no longer be a part-time student and stay-at-home mom. For the first time in many years, I would have coworkers and earn money. I would be viewed in some settings as having a new kind of authority because I had earned a master's degree. I would have to think about practical things like sack lunches and "professional" clothes.

I entered the work force at 38 by taking on several different part-time jobs. At the same time that I was adjusting to life in the working world, I noticed I was also branching out in new areas totally unconnected to my work. Learning contemplative prayer and beginning to write fiction stand out as hugely transforming events for me, deepening my faith in nonverbal and profound ways, giving me new windows through which to look at life and filling my heart with rich and unexpected joy.

I was 45 when I was ordained to serve as an associate pastor in a congregation. The same year I got my first book contract. Many of my questions of purpose and life direction have been answered—for the present! Yet as I have navigated my forties, I have experienced painful losses that came out of the blue, some of which are still perplexing and haunting.

Observers of adult life stages notice that most adults experience a significant transition roughly every seven to ten years. Even for those of us who don't have a midlife crisis, the transitions between 35 and 55 still carry significant weight. Decisions are more complex than they were in early adulthood. We may be weighed down by a mortgage, kids' needs, unexpected health issues or the demands of caring for aging parents. We may have been engaged in one line of work long enough to have our identity and our monthly budget pretty firmly rooted in our career, making change difficult.

Some of us will experience a true midlife crisis, an intense experience of questioning and self-doubt. A MacArthur Foundation study released in 1999 showed that approximately 10 percent of adults experience a midlife crisis. That fits with my anecdotal evidence. I have talked with over a hundred people about their midlife experiences, and only about a dozen talked about a profound and debilitating midlife crisis. Most of the people I interviewed who had experienced a midlife crisis came through it with the same kind of growth and sense of discovery experienced by those of us whose midlife experiences were less intense.

When I listened to people talk about midlife, I was struck by the common themes that lay behind the diverse individual stories. The themes paralleled my own experience. People talked about the variety of losses that pile up during the midlife years. Each loss carries pain of its own, but it's the accumulation of the losses between 35 and 55 that makes them so challenging. I also heard about the discoveries of midlife: new hobbies, new joys, new and fruitful spiritual disciplines, new freedom from "shoulds" and "oughts," and an increased ability to live in the moment and receive grace from God.

You have just heard a little of my midlife story, and you will hear more bits and pieces of it in the chapters to come. You will also be hearing the stories of many more people at midlife. I have changed all the names and some of the identifying details. Occasionally, one of the stories is a composite of two or three people.

If you're one of those midlife folks who feels alone in your experiences, I think you will enjoy hearing the voices of others at midlife. It is fascinating to note the great variety in the individual midlife experiences, coupled with the consistency of the overarching themes.

In the first two chapters of this book, I have tried to present an overview of the kinds of losses and discoveries that I heard people talk about in my interviews. The remaining chapters present specific spiritual disciplines and practices that are helpful at midlife. Some of these practices were very common themes in my interviews. A huge percentage of the people I interviewed talked about their newfound joy in experiencing God's presence in nature. A good number talked about the significance of contemplative prayer, Sabbath-keeping, embracing mystery, relating to God with the heart and visiting Benedictine monasteries.

The chapter on Celtic Christian spirituality comes from my own experience. As I have watched the growing enthusiasm for Celtic music, poetry and spirituality in our culture, and as I have studied the themes of Celtic Christianity, I have become convinced of its relevance for people at midlife and its profound connection to the issues of midlife.

You will notice in this book that when I need to use a pronoun for God, I use "he" or "him." I want to clarify that I do not believe that God is male. The Bible teaches clearly that God is neither male nor female; God is the Lord of gender and cannot be limited to being either male or female. I am also aware that for women who have been abused, the use of a male pronoun for God raises all kinds of difficult issues.

Despite my concern for theological accuracy and pastoral sensitivity, I continue to use male pronouns for God because I care so deeply that we understand God calls us to a personal, intimate relationship. I prefer to speak naturally about God as if he is a vibrant person close to me, and for me that means using the same pronouns I would use for any person I want to be close to. I do want you to know that lots of careful consideration lies behind this decision.

One helpful metaphor for midlife is half time. We are called to pause sometime in the years between 35 and 55 to evaluate the way we have spent the first half of our lives and to prepare for the second half. For cable TV executive Bob Buford, writing in *Half Time: Changing Your Game Plan from Success to Significance*,[1] the years before 35 were all about financial and business success. Then God called him to stop and consider how to live the second half of his life focused more on significance.

In our frantic culture, how can we pause for half time? How can we take time to evaluate the meaning of our lives? How can we find purpose and significance? The people of God have pondered these questions throughout the centuries, and through the spiritual disciplines presented in this book you can find structure to help you pause and seek God's voice.

My prayer for each reader is that, having read this book, you will feel more confident that God is at work in and through the circumstances that characterize your midlife journey. I pray that you will be encouraged to try new spiritual disciplines, and that some of the things you try will give you new enthusiasm for drawing near to God. May these new spiritual disciplines nurture and ground you as you walk fresh paths in the second half of life.

Acknowledgments

First and foremost, I want to thank the dozens of people who talked to me about their experiences at midlife when I was writing my earlier book, *Embracing Midlife: Congregations as Support Systems.*[1] Many of those folks are named in the acknowledgements in that book. Their reflections and experiences shaped my understanding of midlife.

I am also thankful for the people who allowed me to interview them for this book. Some of the interviews focused on personal experience and some on information about the topics of this book. I am grateful to Rev. Dan Baumgartner, Anne Baumgartner, Lesli Corthell, John Hoyte, Don Kunze, Brad Liljequist, Alice Manawelian, Lydia McCauley, Rabbi James Mirel, Marlene Muller, Rev. Bruce Murphy, Pam Tate, and Margie and Jeff Van Duzer. Susan Forshey gave me valuable information for several chapters and looked up some important references for me. Michael Peterson made many valuable suggestions for the chapter on Benedictine spirituality. Five people gave significant time to reading early drafts of the book, and their feedback was very valuable to me: I am grateful to Dan and Anne Baumgartner, Jill Bell, Chris Gustafson, and my always helpful husband, Dave Baab.

1

The Losses of Midlife

Sandi and I were best friends in childhood, but we seldom managed to see each other as adults. In the year that we turned 47, I traveled to her state twice for conferences, and we connected for nice long visits. I met her husband and her grown stepkids, who came to her house for dinner.

In the first visit, we spent a lot of time catching up. By the second visit, we had built up enough trust to go deeper.

"I always wanted to have kids," she told me on the second visit. "Always. But I didn't want to rush into it, partly because I spent so much time caring for my own younger sisters when I was growing up. I knew I needed some space before becoming a parent. So in my twenties I just waited to be ready. In my early thirties I knew I was ready, but I also knew my marriage was falling apart.

"I got a divorce and lived alone for a while. Then I met Sam. I never knew a relationship could be so good. This was a man I knew I could have kids with. When I was 38, I went in for a checkup, and the doctor ordered some blood tests. To my astonishment, they told me my hormone levels showed there was no chance that I could become pregnant.

"I always thought I had plenty of time to have children. No one ever told me a person could go through menopause in their late thirties. It's so common to see actresses having children at 45. No one told me fertility is highest around age 30.

"Every time I realize I will never have children of my own, the sense of loss is immense. I adore my stepkids. I enjoy my job at the high school, where I get to have all kinds of relationships with kids. But it's not the same. I always wanted to have kids of my own. Why didn't anyone tell me to start earlier? The sense of loss never goes away."

Sandi's experience of loss is very different from Jack's. Unlike Sandi, Jack seems to have it all: an attractive wife, two high-achieving teenage children and a high-paying job as an engineer. His forties have been marked by a different kind of sadness.

"All day long I work hard. I know I'm good at what I do, but I am bored out of my mind. I've simply been doing it too long.

"But how can I change careers now? College tuition is right on the horizon. And we're comfortable in our lifestyle. Besides, I can't think of anything I'd rather do. If I had a strong sense of direction, sure, I'd follow it. But I don't. I just slog through the days, waiting for something—I don't know what.

"I feel such a sense of loss. I dreamed of having a happy family and a great job. I love my wife and kids, but where I spend most of my time is at work. I never imagined it would be like this, the numbness, the sense of time passing without meaning."

The Losses Accumulate

During the years between 35 and 55, most people experience a variety of losses. In many cases the losses are unexpected and surprising, the very last thing we would have imagined.

I was 40 when my older son turned 13. As he entered his argumentative teen years, I had to relinquish the myth that I was a perfect mother who had created such a healthy home environment that my kids would always be respectful and appreciative.

I was 42 when one of my closest friends died of a brain tumor. While she was dying, I came down with a very serious lung disease. It took me more than a year to recover completely. Only a couple of years later, my husband's parents died one after the other, and I tried to give him support as he processed the reality of being an orphan. These three events of my forties made me much more aware of the certainty of death than I had ever been before.

In my late forties, I overused my shoulder setting up 450 chairs for an event at church. After months of physical therapy, cortisone shots, heating pads and ice packs, I had rotator cuff surgery. My shoulder is better than it was before the surgery, but not back to normal by any means. It looks like I will never swim crawl stroke again, and I love to swim. Eleven months after the shoulder surgery, I was back at the hospital for knee surgery. Again, my knee is better than it was before the surgery, but I am still adjusting to new limits on activity. Will I be able to go on the long, rambling walks I have always enjoyed? It seems unlikely, and I miss those walks with a sharp and searing pain in my soul.

Each of these losses is painful in itself. And each of these losses could have occurred at any age. What's new at midlife for most people is the way the losses accumulate and build on each other in a bewildering and sometimes overwhelming fashion. At the same time that we face new physical limitations, we may also be dealing with complex family and work transitions. It can feel like too much at once.

The accumulation of these losses can prompt us to grow spiritually, to draw near to God in new ways. As we understand the fragility of life, we grow in humility. As we come up against limitations we couldn't have imagined, we are offered an opportunity to evaluate what is most important to us. The increasing awareness of the reality of death that many experience in their midlife years can be a call to

---

We Grieve for Our Tattered Dreams

We grieve for our youth, for our strong bodies, for the sense that we were needed, for the tattered dreams and ideals that we see no way of mending. Often when we feel we cannot bear another ending, it is pressed upon our lives anyway: a parent's sickness, the death of a friend, a diagnosis of illness. We may be dealing not simply with one major transition, but with many small or larger ones. Even when the event is one we welcome or find relatively easy—as some women do with menopause, retirement, or the leaving home of children—it still involves adjustment.

KATHLEEN FISCHER, *Autumn Gospel*

---

deepen our awareness of the kingdom of God on earth and the reality of heaven on the other side of death. The words of the psalmist become more real: "My flesh and my heart may fail, but God is the strength of my heart and my portion forever" (Ps 73:26).

The losses of midlife offer us an opportunity to grow and discover new things, to reframe and re-center our lives around our deepest values. In effect, we are offered the chance to change course, to adjust our goals and dreams as we enter the second half of life. Midlife has been described as a second adolescence, a second opportunity to grow up, find our own values and chart a course that is uniquely our own.

My Body, My Self

During the midlife years, women lose fertility. Both men and women lose strength and flexibility. For some, these losses are devastating and humiliating. For others, they are mild inconveniences. For almost everyone, they are changes that force themselves into our awareness.

The loss of fertility can be especially painful for women like Sandi who have never had children, whether they are single or married. Some women who have had children also experience deep pain at menopause because it represents the end of a role that they have enjoyed.

John, a physically fit 53-year-old, despises the fact that his body has changed so much. "I could always count on my body," he says. "I have always loved sports and found my greatest joy in being active. The last time I played tennis, I fell when I was chasing a ball. I threw my back out. It was painful for days, and I could barely walk! That kind of thing never happened when I was younger." Even though John stays in excellent shape, the strength, agility and ease of physical activity that he took for granted in his twenties have disappeared.

John also hates to look in the mirror and see a gray-haired man staring back at him. "My body is in good shape—I work out and stay fit. But I can't do anything about my face!"

For many people, the physical changes that come with aging are disconcerting and frustrating. The increase in medical issues can be equally frustrating, whether it's high blood pressure, digestive trouble or a host of other problems. Our bodies require more maintenance and care.

Bifocals, hot flashes, receding hairlines, painful joints, medical "procedures" that are more like small surgeries, fatigue after exertion and memory lapses are reminders that we are moving inexorably toward old age. Some of us can no longer consume caffeine at bedtime and get a decent night's sleep. Some of us can no longer consume caffeine at all! In a culture that worships youth, we are shocked to discover we are no longer young.

Out of this shock we have the opportunity to refocus on what is most important to us. We have the opportunity to draw near to God afresh, to look for our deepest values and live by those values in new ways. Our losses can be a call to reevaluate our lives and center ourselves around God in ways we have never experienced before.

All in the Family

Many single people are in their midlife years when they begin to experience despair over not being married or not having children. Many people are in their midlife years when their children become teenagers and then leave the nest. Many are between 35 and 55 when their parents become incapacitated or die. These transitions can carry heavy emotional weight and precipitate lots of questioning.

"You married people have had a chance to experience your dreams," says Rhonda, 43. "You may not like the way your dreams have turned out, but don't tell me it's the same as what single people experience. We have to face the fact that we'll probably never have our dreams come true. As I move beyond the age where it's likely that I will have my own children, I feel a real emptiness and sadness. Even if I get married someday—and I still hope I will—I'll probably never give birth to children."

"Is that really worse," Susan, 38, responds, "than the pain and sadness that come from having gotten what you wanted and not liking it very much?" Susan loves being a mother to her young children, but she is very unhappy in her marriage. Like many, she dreamed of a happy marriage. Letting go of the dream is very difficult, as is the challenge of figuring out how to nurture her strained marriage and cope with the thoughts of divorce that run through her head.

In our twenties and early thirties, it's easy to be optimistic that things will work out well in our relationships. There's still time to get married if we're not, still time to have children, still the possibility of turning around a difficult relationship. As we move into our late thirties and forties, many experience the sense of time running out, whether the issue is childlessness, a difficult marriage, painful relationships within the extended family, or children who challenge and disappoint us.

Most parents are in their midlife years when they experience the jarring transition from compliant, affectionate child to independent teenager who may desire all kinds of things that seem inappropriate to the parent. Whether parents resist or give in to such bizarre (to us) choices as strange haircuts, tattoos and body piercing, simply entering into discussion about such options raises all kinds of tension. *What happened to the sweet elementary school child I got used to? Where did this temper, these strange opinions, all these emotions come from? I know I liked to stay out late when I was a teenager, but why is my 16-year-old expecting to stay out until 2 a.m. at a party? When I was 16, I had an 11 p.m. curfew.*

Until our children are teenagers, we may have been able to maintain a sense of confidence in our parenting. The presence of teens in our lives can throw that confidence to the winds. We are off balance, unsure of what to do, mourning the loss of the easy days of parenting, which didn't seem easy at the time!

More couples are starting a family in their late thirties, forties or even fifties. They experience the physical changes of midlife while engaged in the early stages of parenthood. "I'm going through menopause and toddlers at the same time," one mid-forties woman moaned. "I'm out of sync with my friends. The ones who have young kids can't talk about menopause, and my friends who can empathize about the changes in my body have teenagers or an empty nest. I don't really fit in anywhere!"

For couples who begin their parenting journey at midlife, or for those who have another child later in life, the joy of parenting is often very real and very sweet. But the fatigue from late nights and the high energy demanded by young children also loom large. Life is very different than it was before kids.

The empty nest, another major transition that happens to many parents during their midlife years, creates another set of losses. Just when the teenagers are becoming easier to live with, they leave. After missing them and feeling sad, we settle into a new pattern of life. Just when that new way of living gets comfortable, the kids are back in the house for a holiday, a short visit or a long stay. We want to welcome them, but we are also aware that we miss the quiet and order that we had begun to enjoy in their absence. The variety of emotions inside ourselves can be baffling and unexpected.

Many people are in their midlife years when their parents' health begins to fail and all sorts of difficult decisions arise. *Should my parents stay in their home? If not, how in the world am I going to convince them to move? What kind of care is best for them? How do I find it? How do I cope with the guilt that I feel because I'm considering putting my parents in a nursing home?*

When a parent dies, grief is often accompanied by a set of unexpected questions and dilemmas. *Now that Mom is gone and no longer cooks for Dad, how can I help him improve his eating habits and choose something other than hot dogs? How can I help Dad cope with his overwhelming sadness without Mom? Or perhaps, How should I respond to Mom's new boyfriend? What should I do now that Mom and her boyfriend have moved in together?*

And when both parents are gone, the complexity of the losses can be even more baffling and overwhelming. In the midst of grief, the estate needs to be settled. Perhaps a house needs to be sold and siblings need to divide up the household goods. Perhaps there are surprises in the will and hurt feelings need to be soothed at the same time that the funeral service is being planned.

My husband was 50 when he lost his father, only three years after his mother died. My husband and his father had always been close, and the sense of loss was much greater than expected, partly because his father's illness came as a surprise. My father-in-law was a healthy man until he got a fast-growing cancer, and we had expected him to live for many more years. Now, five years after his father's death, the feeling of being an orphan continues to surprise my husband. No one expects a man in his fifties to feel like an orphan, but his sense of being alone in the world is very real.

All of these losses around family life precipitate questioning. *Where is God in my difficult family situation? Why has God not given me what I dreamed of, what I longed for? Why didn't God give me a wife [a better relationship with my sister, easier children, a bigger inheritance, a parent who ages gracefully]? How am I going to cope with this difficult situation?* Because many people experience more than one challenge in their family life during the midlife years, many are asking how they are going to cope with the combination of challenges they face.

Loss of Certainty

One of the most subtle losses that often occurs at midlife is a change in one's sense of certainty. When we were 25, we might have felt certain that if society just banded together and worked at it, homelessness could be ended. After ten years of activism around poverty and housing, encountering over and over again the complexities of the issues, the 35-year-old is no longer so certain. The new parents, in their late twenties or early thirties, are sure that if they express enough love to their children, their children will be respectful, healthy and loving. By the time those children are in their late teens, the parents can only be grateful things have gone moderately well. Their children are often respectful and loving, and their lives are relatively healthy, but it was touch and go many times. And the parents are not sure exactly what worked and what didn't work.

This loss of certainty is connected with letting go of the illusion of control. The athlete in his twenties is deeply committed to exercise and fitness. He feels sure that if he continues his regimen, he'll be able to compete the way he wants to. In his thirties, a series of injuries slows him down. He is no longer certain he can reach his goals, and he sees that being driven to accomplish something does not guarantee getting there. He begins to realize that life is simply not completely in his control. Health problems, unexpected financial losses, unpredictable career setbacks and the challenge of parenting are only a few of the ways we learn that we are not in control of everything.

At its best, this move toward relinquishing certainty and control results in greater peace, the ability to enjoy the moment, and the conviction that the only thing to do is trust God with our lives. At its worst, these changes set off a chain of reactions beginning with disillusionment and discouragement and culminating in depression, anxiety and immobilization. I have certainly experienced a mixture of all these emotions and convictions as I have navigated midlife.

I was shocked to discover, over the decade of my thirties, how little of my life is actually in my control. I am naturally organized and a planner, and I believed in my early adult life that if I planned things, they would happen. And I expected that things would happen in a way that I liked! Difficult pregnancies and a major church conflict were only two of the events that contributed to a strong sense that life wasn't turning out the way I expected. I felt disoriented, uncomfortable and off balance as I realized how little control I have and how necessary it is to trust God—rather than my own plans—in the complexities of life.

At the same time that I experienced disillusionment and discouragement because life was beyond my control, a stunning thought began to creep into my awareness. I began to notice that some of the very best things in life come to me unexpectedly. If I'm so busy expecting one thing, I won't even notice these others—gifts of grace, unexpected joys, precious moments that are intensely wonderful, unplanned and oh so fleeting. I am still a person who plans and organizes many parts of my life, but I am learning to rejoice in the grace of unexpected, blessed moments.

I am more certain than ever about the core values of my life: the reality of God's love in Christ, God's call to worship and service, the power of prayer and the wonder of human love. But I am less certain about many other issues that used to get me excited. I have learned that being a fanatic about nutrition does not guarantee perfect health and that trying to be gentle and kind in every setting doesn't eliminate

---

The End of Unlimited Promise

Midlife is the metaphysical point where we recognize the end of unlimited promise and the fact that we cannot control many of the bad things that happen to us. In a de-illusioning period we incorporate those truths, which can weight us down and make us feel prematurely old during the period of transition. But we should also recognize that we do have increasing control over the good things that happen to us. And that is what makes flourishing possible in the forties.

GAIL SHEEHY, *New Passages*

---

all conflicts. I am also much less certain that I can organize and plan my way to a joyful life. I now trust God's guidance and goodness in ways I couldn't have dreamed earlier in my life. The path to that increased level of trust has involved a lot of sadness, discouragement and loss, and I am grateful to be on the other side of that dark pathway, at least for now.

Loss of Illusions About Ourselves

During the first decade or two of adult life, we are often able to convince ourselves that we are fairly honorable, loving, kind and decent human beings. At midlife, we gain access into our inner lives in a new way. This can be very positive and fruitful, as we explore values, meaning and memories. It can also be humiliating.

Part of the task of midlife is to relinquish the illusions we have had about ourselves. Yes, we are sometimes loving, kind and honorable individuals. Other times we are deeply tempted to return evil for evil, to fight back vindictively rather than returning a gentle answer, and to give in to inappropriate sexual desires. All those forces—good and evil—are inside us. This is what the Bible affirms about humanity, and it is humiliating to find out how true it is.

We can find in our inner life a desire for violence and retribution that is stunning in its intensity. Sexual fantasies, rather than declining with age, seem to get more vivid. Anger, vindictiveness, fear and petty desires can all come to the surface at midlife in a way we never expected. The passages in the Psalms where the psalmist wants to kill his enemies seem all too relevant. The maturity and godliness we thought we'd have at this age seem out of reach.

It can be very freeing to admit the truth about ourselves. We can come to God in prayer more sincerely and with far greater compassion for others when we are honest about the mix of good and bad motives we find in ourselves. We realize our need for community to support us in doing good and fleeing evil. We grow in humility and softness as we realize that we're not God's gift to the universe—we're simply flawed individuals like everyone else.

Unresolved Issues from the Past

Another subtle but real area that sometimes surfaces at midlife involves issues from the past. Midlife truly is a second opportunity to grow up: to affirm our own values rather than the values of our parents, to consider again what we learned in childhood and decide what we want to keep and what we want to leave behind. A part of this process of reevaluation involves looking at our childhood experiences with fresh eyes. Many of us will find unresolved issues that will need to be pondered afresh. The increased reflection that is natural after 35 gives us the opportunity to look at our past and seek healing for the difficult parts.

Ron was physically abused by his father and then, in his late teens, he was sexually abused by a church youth leader. In his twenties Ron had some brief counseling and tried to set aside all his pain and get on with his life. To some extent he was successful, and his thirties were characterized by job success. But in his forties he found he needed to revisit the whole mess.

An encounter with the youth leader who had abused him set off an intense period of reevaluation and depression. With the help of the pastors at his church, he got extensive counseling. He was on an antidepressant medication for a period of time. Now, in his late forties, he experiences healing and peace to a degree that could not have happened in his twenties and thirties when he was trying to ignore what had happened to him. He had to face his pain, his losses, in a fresh way in order to move toward health.

For Julia, the emerging sexuality of her teenage daughters made her unable to ignore any longer the impact of her family's inappropriate sexual talk that had so frequently made her feel uncomfortable as a child. Julia has been in a very supportive and helpful women's group for several years. As her daughters have grown up, she has grown up too, facing the remnants of her childhood in her life today. She is more clear about her own desires and more at peace as a child of her heavenly Father than she has ever been. She sees more clearly what her parents' values were, and she understands better which of those values she wants to keep and which ones she would like to jettison. She credits the support of the group.

Many people at midlife are surprised to find that issues from the past simply aren't finished. Whether it's an intense romantic relationship from many years ago or a pattern of childhood conflict with a parent, memories and emotions force themselves on our awareness, and we need to expend energy figuring out the best way to cope with them. People at midlife report many different practices that give them time and space for this kind of life review: counseling, journaling, contemplative prayer, walking in nature, joining support groups. Inner healing prayer—where we ask God to enter into painful memories and heal them—can bring resolution. God, the giver of soothing balm for our souls, enters into our lives in new ways as we face old wounds.

One of the helpful metaphors for midlife is a tree. In Psalm 1 we are encouraged to draw near to God and be like trees planted by streams of water. To use this picture of a tree to understand midlife, think of the whole of your life as a tree. In the first half of life, we are

---

Midlife Healing

There are certain aspects of healing that need to be a part of midlife growth: acknowledging the wounds and accompanying emotions, recognizing their source, being compassionate toward ourselves, letting go and being less in control, forgiving self and others, facing our fears, developing a sense of humor, surrendering to a divine presence greater than ourselves, and being patient with how slowly healing often happens while also being attentive to and caring for our body, mind, and spirit.

JOYCE RUPP, *Dear Heart, Come Home*

---

growing branches and learning to produce fruit, all the visible aspects of growth and health. As we begin the second half of life, we find we need to spend some effort tending the roots, the unseen parts of our lives. Are the roots well nourished? Are they placed near sources of water and nutrients? Does the ground around the roots need weeding or other special care? We realize that the branches of the tree cannot keep growing and producing fruit if the roots are not well tended.

Many at midlife find that they need to take a break from bearing fruit in order to give attention to their roots, their unseen self. This might involve a sabbatical from teaching Sunday school or a leave of absence from singing in the choir. The restless fatigue that calls us to take a break from service and ministry can also be a call to focus on the roots of the tree that is our life. A week at a monastery, a contemplative prayer group, a new commitment to exercise or an art class may be a way for you to tend your inner being—the roots of your life—so that good fruit can be produced in the future.

The Messengers of Midlife

It's very common for people at midlife to find that tears are a companion on the journey. Also common at midlife is increased sleeplessness. Several writers on midlife call these "messengers of midlife." These messengers call us to pay attention to the roots of the tree, to nurture the unseen parts of our lives.

Other messengers of midlife include illness, depression, weight loss or gain, marital problems, divorce, impotence, job loss or dissatisfaction and fatigue. Thank heaven one person won't have all of these! One or more of these messengers is an indication that some attention needs to be paid to the deeper things of life.

In his book on men at midlife, Methodist minister James Harnish describe what midlife often feels like by using the metaphor of steering through the detours.[1] Whether it's job loss or marital problems, tears or sleeplessness, the messengers of midlife seem to be leading us on a detour away from the life we planned. Whether it's infertility or rebellious teenagers, arthritis or unfinished issues from childhood, the losses, transitions, and bewilderment of these years can make us feel that we are detouring from what's really important.

The theme of this book is that God desires to use the detours to help us deepen in faith and grow in our ability to love and serve. In order to grow at midlife and establish patterns that will take us through the second half of life in a healthy and wise manner, we need grow in our ability to view all these "detours" as means of discovery, things God can use to teach us what we need to know in order to draw closer to him. The messengers of midlife can be a part of that call to growth.

One woman reports that her doctor gave her considerable reassurance as she began to experience sleepless nights. He told her to expect that sleeping through the night would become a thing of the past. He said that he often awakens around 3:00 a.m. but simply doesn't worry about it. He has developed a peaceful routine. He gets up, climbs into his recliner with a blanket, prays for a while, then reads until he feels sleepy and can drift off.

This doctor has found a way to cope with the loss of confidence that he will usually sleep through the night. Part of the task of midlife is to cope creatively with the various messengers. I always carry tissues with me now because I am so much more likely to get tears in my eyes at the most unexpected times. We can look for positive ways to respond to the "detours" we encounter.

In the next chapter, we will see the variety of discoveries that people at midlife make—a wide range of new and fresh hobbies, spiritual practices and ways of looking at the world that can begin for us in the midlife years. Often those life-giving discoveries come out of the simple need for relief from the pain of all the losses. Whether it's taking a moment to enjoy the spring flowers or rediscovering a musical instrument, God provides countless opportunities to draw near and experience his grace and goodness. The pain and challenges of midlife can enable us to appreciate the small gifts and blessed opportunities that we didn't really notice in the first half of life.

Questions for Reflection

To think about, write about or talk about with friends.

1. Make a list of the losses you have experienced in your life. Which losses still affect you today? What is their impact in your life?

2. In what ways have you experienced loss of certainty, loss of the illusion of control or loss of illusions about yourself? How do you feel about these losses? Spend some time praying about these losses.

3. In what ways have your losses made it hard to feel close to God? Have the losses drawn you closer to God in any way? Are there new ways you would like to draw near to God in the midst of loss?

2

The Discoveries of Midlife

John took a watercolor painting class when he was 50. Now, three years later, he finds that he looks at the world differently. When he sees towering clouds, bright on top and stormy gray at the bottom, he thinks about how he could paint the darkness and the light. He looks at trees, flowers and mundane household objects intently, noticing the variation in color and the effect of shadows.

As he observes all these details in the physical world, he feels close to God, the Creator of everything he sees. When he paints, whether he's alone or with a friend, he experiences an intense joy. That kind of joy was missing from his life throughout the decade of his forties.

John was 43 when he reached his career goal of tenure at a large university. Things went downhill from there. He had thought tenure would earn him the respect of his peers, but they seemed just as indifferent to his opinion as they had before his promotion. He hadn't realized that his department chair had been protecting him from onerous assignments for several years so he could do research to get tenure. After the big tenure event, his chair piled on him countless boring committee assignments and organizational tasks within the department.

He spent the next few years agonizing about his work, considering leaving the university, but continually returning to the strong sense of call from God he had experienced when he began to teach. He didn't see how he could possibly leave the university when he knew God had called him to teaching. Yet the lack of collegiality with his peers continued to get worse, John became depressed, and his wife got irritated with his continual complaining about work. His kids entered adolescence and stunned John with their bursts of self-absorption and rudeness. Life was absolutely no fun at all, and he had no idea how to receive guidance from God in the midst of the darkness and numbness inside him.

Finally John realized he had to get out of teaching or his whole life would collapse. At 46, he began his own business, working endless hours to get on his feet. Finally, when he was 50, things were established well enough so that he could cut back his work hours. He began to exercise again. He took up weight lifting and finds great satisfaction in his newfound strength. His kids are mostly out of the nest, and he and his wife have a wonderful time exploring parks and eating in new restaurants. He became a deacon in his congregation and finds joy in serving people in need.

And he draws and paints. His absorption with shape, color and light gives him an almost mystical connection with God that he has never experienced before. When he sketches or paints, he is creating alongside the Creator.

Finding

Midlife is all about coping with loss and uncertainty, as we saw in the first chapter. John certainly had his share of loss. He had to let go of the dream that he would be a world-class teacher, appreciated by students and colleagues alike. He had to relinquish his sense of call to teaching, and he had to look for God's guidance into new areas. Like most parents of adolescents, he had to let go of the dream that his children would respect and admire him every moment of their lives. Both of his parents died when he was in his late forties, trying to get his business established. Even though he was almost 50, a grown-up responsible adult, he felt acutely the loss of his parents and the vulnerability of not having in his family a generation older than himself.

John's story illustrates that during the midlife years we not only have to learn to face losses, we also get to experience the surprise of finding new pleasures, new joys and new ways of connecting with God. John's zestful enjoyment of painting and drawing parallels the experience of many midlife folks who take up creative writing, quilting, sewing, woodworking, gardening and dozens of other creative endeavors.

John had always been good at drawing, and he had frequently drawn sketches for handouts in his university classes. He had always wanted to learn to paint, so his foray into watercolors fulfilled an old dream that had been in the back of his mind all his life. This, too, is common at midlife. Many people revive a dream or rediscover a passion from much earlier in their lives.

John's new involvement as a deacon illustrates another common midlife experience: finding new avenues of service. Some of these new avenues may be the fulfillment of a dream from long ago, but they also may be completely fresh, different and unexpected. Whether it's playing with kids in the church nursery or repairing hiking trails, a new and different place to serve can emerge at midlife and bring great joy.

Many folks find new and intense pleasure in the physical world. This may involve sheer enjoyment of creation, in part like John's experience of intense analysis when he looks at clouds, trees and flowers. It may take the form of a new expression with the physical body. John's pleasure in his increasing strength and visible muscles is a common experience during the midlife years. Dancing, walking, hiking, biking and kayaking are forms of exercise that midlife people frequently describe with enthusiasm.

John's almost mystical experience of God through the visual beauty of creation parallels the experience of many. God is indeed knowable in Jesus Christ, yet God also dwells in unimaginable glory and majesty. At midlife, many find themselves more connected with the wonder and mystery of God. We don't have to understand everything about God in order to worship; in fact, as we get older we

---

A Quickening of Reverence

The task in this transition is not only psychological; it is also spiritual. There is a quickening of reverence in the presence of art and nature, as almost everyone begins to wonder where he or she might fit in the larger scheme of things. We sense that time is growing short and there is no use waiting to settle old scores. It's time to forgive the erring parent, embrace the estranged sibling, let go of disappointments in the prodigal child. Religious faith may be reconsidered or renewed.

GAIL SHEEHY, *New Passages*

---

become more aware that we cannot possibly understand everything about God's ways and God's power. At midlife, many find themselves comforted by the increasing awareness of just how huge and awesome God is.

In this chapter, we will explore the variety of ways people at midlife find new pleasures, new challenges and new ways of experiencing God.

The Physical World

Psalm 19 has taken on increased significance for me at midlife. "The heavens are telling the glory of God; and the firmament proclaims his handiwork," writes the psalmist. "Day to day pours forth speech, and night to night declares knowledge" (Ps 19:1-2). It is amazing the way the creation speaks to me in new ways about God's glory. I so easily find myself praying along with these words from Psalm 104: "O LORD, how manifold are your works! In wisdom you have made them all; the earth is full of your creatures" (Ps 104:24). The reds and pinks of sunsets, the blazing fall leaves, the tender greens of spring, the shape of a tree silhouetted against the bright winter sky . . . for me and for many people at midlife, all of these seem rich and endowed with meaning in a way they never have before.

A significant number of people find themselves surprised at the way their own creative activities help them feel connected to God the Creator. For many of the people who talked with me about midlife, new creative outlets have emerged in their late thirties and forties, and these activities have an unexpected spiritual significance.

I was 39 when I began writing fiction. It took me almost a year to write my first short story, but the next several stories came pretty quickly. I then wrote a short novel and several longer ones. By the time I was in my mid-forties, I had switched to nonfiction book writing, and I actually found success in having my writing published.

I sometimes wonder if I will ever return to fiction writing, but whether or not I do, I will never forget the exhilaration of those first few years of writing stories. I felt I was creating right alongside God, who created the universe out of nothing. I was creating stories using words that I had no hand in creating, but the characters and the plots came out of nowhere. I had dreamed them up myself, just like God dreamed up the universe. I don't know why that experience was so powerful and awesome, but I do know that many other people have described similar feelings connected with creative activities.

One of my friends makes beautiful scrapbooks of family photos. Another finds great pleasure in decorating her home and planning new fences and flower beds for her yard. Someone else makes quilted wall hangings. Another friend writes poetry. I know a social worker who finds balance for his intense work through making beautiful furniture in his workshop. For many, these creative endeavors enable a connection with God the Creator in new ways.

Physical exercise is another way in which people at midlife experience connection with God the Creator. Quite a few folks told me the ways they have been surprised at the feeling of spiritual significance they have experienced as they have learned to use their bodies in new ways.

At 37, Carrie began to participate in dance lessons. She learned a kind of modern dance in which a variety of emotions are expressed by the body. As a very verbal and insightful person, she had always enjoyed talking with people about emotions. She found a new kind of insight and freedom in the nonverbal expression of emotions through dance.

At 46, Rea has also begun to take dance classes, in her case ballroom dance. After a difficult divorce and many years in banking, Rea realized she lives almost entirely in the cognitive realm. The ballroom dancing enables her to meet people, but most important, she is beginning to get reconnected to her body in a way that she hasn't experienced since she was a child. God made us as physical beings, and the rediscovery of the joy of physical expression is part of midlife for many folks.

My mother took up both golf and downhill skiing in her forties, and now, in her seventies, she continues to participate enthusiastically in both. She loves getting outside in the sun and wind, seeing the beauty of the snow in the mountains and the variety in weather and seasons on the golf course. She is a wonderful model of the truth that at midlife one of our tasks is to discover patterns of living that will endure through the second half of our lives and give us pleasure, joy and connection with God in new ways.

Unfulfilled Dreams

Rob, in his mid-forties, has a ponytail. He's been growing it for a couple of years and it continues to get longer. He can't bring himself to cut it off because he has always dreamed of having a ponytail. He just never got around to it until he reached his forties.

Rob's hair may seem a trivial example of a long-held dream that has finally come to life, but he gets a real kick out of it. His long hair represents something significant to him—a commitment to be a little different from his culture and the people around him.

Perhaps a part of Rob's enthusiasm for his long hair comes from a realization that hits so many people in their forties. We realize that if we don't begin to pursue our dreams now, we will never get around to them. In our twenties and early thirties, we usually feel that we have all the time in the world. In our forties and fifties, as we face the fact that we will one day die—one of the losses most midlife folks find themselves acknowledging. We realize that our time on earth is finite and we need to start pursuing those old dreams.

Many of the creative endeavors or physical activities that people take up during the midlife years are indeed a fulfillment of an earlier dream. Changing careers, going back to school, adopting a child or having a baby, taking up golf, providing day care for a grandchild, traveling overseas, learning to play the piano . . . all of these activities have been described to me as the fulfillment of a long-held dream, and all can be deeply meaningful, true gifts from God.

The Fruits of Turning Inward

At midlife many people report increased joy in being alone. This can take the form of quiet devotional activities, such as journaling, establishing a place to pray in the home, walking alone and praying, observing the Sabbath in quiet, or praying quietly in an empty church. Many midlife folks find increased joy in being alone in the home doing domestic tasks or reading. The intent of those activities is not prayer, yet a spirit of companionship with God may be more common than ever before.

The turn inward that is so common at midlife also often manifests itself as increased desire to think about our lives. *Have I made the most of my life so far? Did I accomplish what I set out to do? What changes do I need to make as I move into the second half of life?*

As we saw in the first chapter, so many of the illusions of the first half of life are falling away. It becomes clear that we may never be as

---

A Garden Within Me

Like the children [in the film The Secret Garden*] discovering a much-neglected place of beauty, in midlife I had found a garden within me that needed attention and was not beginning to bloom. Like the children, I had found the key to this place and had given much inner work to weeding and planting. When the flowers in the film began to bloom, I felt those flowers come to life inside of me. They gave me a huge sense of hope and promise, confirming the value of my midlife journey as a source of personal transformation.*

JOYCE RUPP, *Dear Heart, Come Home*

---

successful or as beautiful as we imagined. *This is my life*, I find myself thinking, *and it's the only life I'm going to get. How can I make the most of it?*

Often people in their forties and fifties begin to drop the masks that have hid their true selves for the first half of life. This comes about in part because of the many questions about meaning and value that arise at midlife. We may realize that desperately trying to make a good impression is no longer as important to us as when we were younger. Dropping masks can help us experience greater honesty in prayer and in conversations. We can find increased peace with God and increased acceptance of who we are.

Julia has vivid memories of the church of her childhood. She believes that masks were continually encouraged by a general attitude that everything negative needed to be covered up. She learned to put on a cheerful, superficially content expression at all times.

Midlife has brought many questions for Julia. As she has turned inward in prayer and reflection, she has found great growth in the discipline of trying to be honest with God. Exercising this discipline year after year in her forties, she has begun to experience peace with God and openness with her family and friends in a way she never experienced before. It has taken a lot of commitment and work for Julia to embrace honesty. It definitely doesn't come naturally to her. But the fruits have been life-giving.

One of the many paradoxes of midlife is connected to this turn inward that is so common at midlife: the simultaneous growth of independence and interdependence. As they focus more on their inner life and experience more contentment in being alone, midlife folks often find an increased sense of independence and confidence in who they are. They find resilience and strength in themselves that surprises them. At the same time, they are growing in their awareness of the ways we need support and care from the people around us. We are not lonely planets; we are part of a web of interconnected relationships.

Julia couldn't have grown at midlife without the support group she has participated in for the past few years. The group has nurtured her in her desire to grow in honesty with God as she faced childhood pain and disillusionment. The women in the group have loved her, shared their own pain with her, prayed with her and given her the opportunity to support them as they supported her. Yet she finds strength and independence in herself in new ways as she receives healing from God and as she grows in honesty with God.

Independence and interdependence—surprising simultaneous fruits of growth and discovery in the midlife years.

The Paradoxes of Midlife

Many people at midlife experience a new sense of the balance of opposites in their lives. Work and rest, time alone and time with people, a growing sense of freedom coupled with a greater commitment to discipline . . . all of these are reported by people at midlife with a bemused sense of humor and irony. Life is full of paradox. Just at the moment when we think we know ourselves, we discover something that feels totally new as we undertake a new job. Just when we feel the most settled and even a little bored in our family life, a totally new path of service lights up our lives.

John had been asked to serve as a deacon in his church off and on throughout his thirties and forties. By the time he finally said yes, he had turned 50. He loves almost everything about being a deacon. It suits his gifts of service and compassion very well. Sometimes he regrets that he didn't agree to be deacon earlier, but he remembers those years of struggling to get his career established while raising young children. He had enough on his plate in those years.

Certainly some people in their forties and even fifties have young children and time-consuming careers. Many people, however, are beginning to have time for new pursuits for the first time in many years. An increased sense of self-knowledge and self-acceptance, coupled with a spirit of adventure, also flows into new patterns of service. Many are surprised at the sense of discovery and joy that they find as they experiment. In her forties, my mother began to volunteer with hospice. Several decades later, she's still involved with hospice and feels deep gratitude for all she has learned there.

Many at midlife make career changes and find that same sense of discovery and joy—in the midst of a great deal of hard work—in their new career choices. In his forties, a pastor leaves the ministry and becomes an AIDS educator. Another person in his forties sells his public relations firm and goes to work for a relief and development agency. A high school teacher enters a Ph.D. program in her forties and becomes a college professor. Each of these people talks with energy and enthusiasm about the choice to try something new.

At the same time, the complexity of life at midlife requires a new look at rest and recreation. As fatigue—from such diverse causes as insomnia, increased stress, teenage kids' late nights—becomes more of a constant companion, the necessity for conscious choices around rest becomes more significant.

Jan, a very social and energetic nurse, began to observe the Sabbath in her forties. She takes one day each week to be alone, spending time reading, praying, thinking and just being. For the first forty years of her life, she could sustain her high-energy lifestyle with lots of contacts with family and friends, but after 40 she began to find she could no longer go at full speed seven days each week.

The benefits of Jan's Sabbath observance go deeper than just physical rest. She realizes that her pattern of life at a fast pace had elements of compulsiveness. As she has taken more time to rest from work and social commitments, she has found she is more able to rest in God. She is more able to affirm that God loves us for who we are, not what we do.

In the midst of constant activity, we may give cognitive assent to the truth that God loves us for who we are, but it is very difficult to believe that truth on a deep level if we are terrifically busy doing things all the time. The development of consistent patterns of rest can help us relax into the truth of God's love for us. We grow in our ability to simply rest in God.

So this is another of the rich paradoxes of midlife growth. At the same time as we grow in finding work and service that are meaningful and that connect more with who we are, we may also grow in our willingness to embrace the necessity for rest. We will act out, in a more healthy manner, the tension between being and doing. Who we are and what we do will become more integrated and connected. The rewards of rest—the ability to know we are loved by God for who we are—will spill over into work and service. This is a great and wonderful gift.

Knowledge and Mystery

"I'm not sure of very much any more," says Kate, 47. "The upheavals of the past decade—deaths in the family, argumentative teenagers, career changes—have shaken me up. I still know God loves me and still believe that love is the center of everything. But I used to be so sure of so many things. On my best days, I'm content to let God be in charge, content to rest in his control and authority. I just don't have to know and understand everything."

Kate is not alone in feeling less certain about many things than she used to feel in her twenties and early thirties. All of us see how complex life is at every level; for lots of things there are no answers. And many midlife folks report increased awareness of the mystery behind what we know of God. So much of what God does and who God is lies beyond our understanding.

Yet we can know God in Jesus Christ, and we can take comfort in his care, provision and protection. This tension between knowledge and mystery is yet one more paradox that can provoke the questioning which is common at midlife. This paradox can also enable people to find a peace they never knew before, as they learn wonder and awe. God is so much bigger than we can describe or imagine. We learn to take our place as dependent creatures and beloved children.

This ability to embrace mystery connects with the other areas of discovery that we have discussed in this chapter. In the midlife years we may begin to experience in new ways God's presence in creation and in creative endeavors. How is God present in the creation? We don't have to understand it all; it is enough to acknowledge the reality that God feels present there for us as we enjoy his physical world and as we engage in creative activities.

This awareness of mystery enables us to face our past more realistically. We won't know everything that motivated our parents and the other key people in our lives. We can't possibly understand everything that ever happened to us. It is enough to know that God cares about all our past pain. It is enough that God is our healer who helps us live each day and who holds us in the palm of his hand.

At midlife, faith becomes much more than a list of statements to believe. As we focus more on our relationship with the knowable yet unknowable God, we need time alone to reflect, ponder and pray. The drive to turn inward, so common at midlife, nurtures and is nurtured by this growing awareness of mystery. The sense of mystery calls us to be quiet in rest and awe in God's presence. The more we do that, the more aware we are of mystery.

The tension between being and doing also feeds into this sense of mystery. God calls us to rest and abide in him as our highest calling. Yet he also calls us to a life of obedience and service. How can these both be true at once? At midlife we embrace more deeply the rhythms of life that call us to service and rest at different times—each at the right time.

Rest, peace, simplicity, joy . . . all these are more real as we grow in our ability to slow down and quietly embrace the mystery that exists in God, who is knowable in Jesus Christ and yet dwells in splendor beyond our imagining.

Fresh Paths

The natural pattern during all our lives is to learn new things and grow in new ways. This growing and learning are often intensified during the midlife years, because during those years people often find themselves evaluating the first half of their lives as they prepare to enter the second half. Reevaluation naturally lends itself to experimentation, discovery and new joys. In this chapter we've seen a small sampling of the many creative outlets and fresh paths that people discover at midlife: watercolor painting, dancing, writing fiction, being in a support group, keeping the Sabbath and enjoying the Creator's handiwork.

Some of the new patterns of connection with God will happen spontaneously. A friend invites Ken to attend an exercise class. It

---

The Beauty of Aging

The Japanese have an adjective for the beauty of aging: shibui. *We have no comparable word in English to capture the distinctive character revealed with age. We find it in the contrast between young saplings and old trees in a forest. The shapes of young . . . trees are straight and symmetrical, often so similar that they are indistinguishable. Old trees, bearing the furrows and scars of centuries, have a unique beauty. There are no two alike.*

KATHLEEN FISCHER, *Autumn Gospel*

---

feels good to stretch his muscles regularly. After a year he realizes that he feels more at home in his body than ever before. Ken senses God's pleasure in the way God made him. Ken feels healthier and more energetic, which he experiences as a gift from God. Ken finds himself walking through his neighborhood more often, praying as he walks. He has fallen into a new habit that works well for him, one that nurtures his spiritual life in unexpected ways. It happened without a lot of effort or intentional choice from him.

Like Ken, we may find ourselves "falling into" fruitful new habits. In addition, we can consciously and deliberately choose to experiment with new patterns of spiritual discipline. Midlife is a natural time for experimentation, as we are drawn to consider how to navigate the second half of life.

I want to encourage a spirit of lightness and humor as we experiment. Let's consider Susan, who can sense herself longing for more silence and quiet in her life, so she starts attending contemplative prayer events. She tries to learn the various patterns of contemplative prayer and strives to look for the hand of God in her life through quiet prayer. She tries to meditate on the Scriptures. She tries hard. Really hard.

But nothing happens. She still finds her most significant connection with God in the structured Bible study she attends every week. She just doesn't experience anything when she tries contemplative prayer.

But one day she wanders in a quilt exhibit, and she decides to study quilting. She goes to exhibits of quilts, reads books on quilting, and begins to sew a small quilt. She finds new joy and creativity in fabric stores, looking at all the beautiful colors, textures, and designs in fabric. When she sees a beautifully made quilt, she marvels at the creativity of the person who made it, paralleling the creativity of the one Creator. She begins to experiment with quilt designs herself, and senses herself creating alongside the Creator.

Not everyone will thrive with contemplative prayer, and not everyone experiences God's creativity in a fabric store! Maybe for you God will be present in a new way on the golf course, in a twelve-step group, in a structured Bible study class, or as you serve in the food bank. But how will we find these new ways to connect with God unless we experiment?

I long for Christians to embrace an attitude that encourages exploration and expectation. This attitude is vitally important at midlife, so we can find the freshness we crave. We have lived a couple of decades of adult life, full of hard work, challenges, disappointments and accomplishments. Now is the time to experiment with new patterns of spiritual practice, so we can grow closer to God in fresh, new ways.

Questions for Reflection

To think about, write about or talk about with friends.

1. Think back on the past two or three years. What have you done or experienced that has been new or different? What have you enjoyed in those new things? What have you learned? What has been

challenging about the new things? Spend some time thanking God for new things and praying about the challenges.

2. Finish this sentence: "I've always dreamed of . . ." Is there any way you could act on that dream?

3. Think of the various hobbies and activities of people you know. Have you ever experienced envy of any of those activities? Could you try any of those things?

For Further Reading

Bob Buford. *Half Time: Changing Your Game Plan from Success to Significance.* Grand Rapids, Mich.: Zondervan, 1994.

Kathleen Fischer. *Autumn Gospel: Women in the Second Half of Life.* New York: Paulist, 1995.

Joyce Rupp. *Dear Heart, Come Home: The Path of Midlife Spirituality.* New York: Crossroad, 1997.

Gail Sheehy. *New Passages: Mapping Your Life Across Time.* New York: Ballantine, 1995.

3

Finding God in All of Life
Celtic Christian Spirituality

A few years ago, a friend from Ireland gave me a book full of pictures from the Book of Kells. I was astonished at the beauty and complexity of the illustrations. It was my first introduction to Celtic Christianity.

The Book of Kells is a lavishly illustrated version of the four Gospels, produced in Ireland between the seventh and ninth centuries. Capital letters are colorful figures of people or animals, intertwined with Celtic knots, those crossed lines with no beginning or end that we see so often today in Celtic jewelry.

There are animals everywhere in the Book of Kells. Fish swim between lines of text; rabbits and mice scamper between the lines. The artists clearly had a deep fondness for God's creatures. A lightness and exuberance characterize every page of the Book of Kells, along with a joy in nature and artistry. These are typical characteristics of Celtic Christianity.

Jan's Story

Jan, 58, spent a year in Britain when she was in her late forties. It was a transforming experience in many ways.

*   *   *

In my forties I was running my own consulting business, my husband was an engineer and our adult children had left home. A minister friend said to me that midlife is a time to take out your values and re-examine them. That certainly happened to me.

I began to question everything: my values, my work, my lifestyle, my relationship with God, my spiritual path. There was a dryness in my faith and in my life. My faith was mostly in my head, not a full-body kind of worship, as the Celts would say.

I kept coming across the phase, "follow your bliss." I always answered, "I'd like to live in England and Scotland for a year." All my life I have wanted to live in Britain and research women in the early Christian church, photograph English villages and visit my extensive family.

A friend gave me good advice, telling me to journal about my dreams and daydreams. I realized as I dreamed that I really wanted my life to be an adventure well lived, and not just by rote and habit, which is the easy way when things are going well. I knew I didn't want just any adventure, but I longed for an adventure with God, for my life to be renewed and transformed.

There were huge obstacles to going: the house, the cats, the 190-pound Newfoundland dog, my husband's business and my own consulting business. But one by one the obstacles melted away, and we found ourselves on our way to England.

My cousins in England and Scotland found us two cottages to

rent. When we first got there, neither cottage was ready so we traveled for five weeks. With no agenda, praying for guidance for the day, we had to simply be open to what we were given. People continually gave us ideas where to go next.

We visited all kinds of sites that are significant to Celtic history: Holy Island, Whitby, Iona, St. David's, Durham, Glastonbury, abbeys and cathedrals as well as ancient sacred sites. In many of these settings I could feel a sense of sacredness, a sense of place, a connection with the ancestors.

I went to a conference led by Esther de Waal. One night she gave a talk on Celtic Christian spirituality. A huge light bulb went on in my head. I realized, "I've been on a Celtic pilgrimage! That's why I'm here. This is the path God has set out for me."

During the rest of our time in England, we visited and revisited Celtic sites. By now I was listening to my whole body. In cathedrals, I would touch the stones. I would hug those stone Celtic crosses or standing stones in fields. The Celtic sites gave me a sense of time and timelessness, a connection with the early Celtic saints. I realized their incredible relevance for us today.

As we returned to the States, I realized I had gained a sense of balance that I never had before. I would look at something and say, "That's God's awesome design," and I would marvel. I have chickens now, and I experience God's amazing creativity in my hens each day: their itty bitty eyelashes, the variety of feathers on different parts of their body. God designed each feather, each eyelash, just right for its function. As I look at the wonder of nature, I realize I'm part of this whole.

There's part of me that has become a mystic or a monk. I value a quiet spiritual walk and meditation. The Celts taught me through the way they prayed: their sense of sacredness, the way they prayed for protection against evil, their awareness of being surrounded by angels. My values have changed so much.

*   *   *

Who Were the Celts?

The Celts were tribal people who can be traced as early as 500 B.C. in France and Germany. The Roman Empire pushed some of the tribes north and west to Great Britain. Within Britain, the Romans pushed them yet further north and west.

Christianity began to come to the British Isles in the second and third centuries after Christ. In the fifth century, St. Patrick was one of many people who brought the Christian faith to Ireland. Because the Christian faith flourished within the already existing Celtic culture, and because the Celtic lands were so far from Rome, Celtic Christianity had a unique flavor and emphasis.

What we call "Celtic Christianity" flourished from about the fifth to ninth centuries throughout the British Isles, but particularly concentrated in the west and north: Cornwall, Wales, Scotland and Ireland. There were also Celts in Brittany in France. Today these lands often host Celtic festivals, drawing musicians and artists who celebrate all things Celtic, both Christian and pre-Christian. In this chapter, we will look specifically at the unique flavor of Christianity as we believe it was practiced in Celtic lands from the middle to the end of the first millennium.

The Celts were described briefly in Greek literature in the centuries before and after Jesus, but very little is known about the pre-Christian Celts. We do know that in the Roman Empire the Celts were renowned for their ability to learn very long stories and poems from memory. Much of what we know about Celtic Christianity we have learned through the poems, prayers, blessings and ballads that have been passed down through the generations in Celtic lands. For centuries, probably ever since the time of Patrick, Celtic children learned about God from the words of their mothers and fathers as they sang softly while cooking, sewing, farming and caring for animals.

In the early twentieth century, traveling salesman Alexander Carmichael visited the highlands and islands of Scotland. He wrote down and published six volumes of Celtic "hymns and incantations" in the collection entitled *Carmina Gadelica*.

I can imagine myself as a woman living in Ireland or Scotland 1,200 or 1,500 years ago. As I set off on a short journey to visit my parents in a neighboring village, I sing to myself a blessing for my journey:

The guarding of the God of life be upon me,
The guarding of loving Christ be upon me,
The guarding of the Holy Spirit be upon me,
    Each step of the way,
To aid me and enfold me,
    Each day and night of my life.[1]

I can also picture myself as a mother or grandmother of young children in Celtic times. As I mend clothes by the firelight in the evening, I sing a soft song that the children can hear as they fall asleep close by. I sing it every night, and the children know it as well as I do. One of them sings along with me:

Christ with me sleeping,
    Christ with me waking,
Christ with me watching,
    Every day and night.[2]

Celtic Christians had a vivid sense of the supernatural, and they cultivated places and times of year when the supernatural world seemed most close to our world. The Celts loved pilgrimages to places where God felt close. They were comfortable with experiencing mystery and awe in the face of a transcendent God. They loved the Trinity: three in one, one in three.

The Celtic Sense of Place

Celtic Christians found God everywhere, in the smallest, most mundane household activity, in nature, and in sites where something special had happened to a saint. They saw every good thing as a gift from God, and they saw difficult experiences as a different kind of gift, a way to learn or a call to repentance.

The fire that warmed the hearth and lightened the darkness also spoke clearly that God is light. The bread that filled the hungry belly spoke of God's provision. The trees and animals spoke of

---

All Is Holy

For the Celtic Christians, God was at hand, and their relationship with God was an intimate one. . . . These were men and women who grasped the true significance of the incarnation, the full reality of a God who became truly human, like us in all things but sin. . . . So because the Celts understood God's presence in and through the created world, for them there was no dualism. Nothing was seen as secular. All was holy, or potentially so. Thus, if all of life is holy, all the pieces which make up the mystery of each of our lives are sacred pieces. Patching them together yields the holy.

JOHN MIRIAM JONES, *With an Eagle's Eye*

God's artistry and care for creation. They saw God clearly in nature. By no means were they pantheists, equating the creation with God. Instead, they understood that the supernatural realm is very close to the physical realm; in fact they believed in and experienced the spiritual world touching our world in certain places. They had a name for the places and times where the spiritual world was most near: "thin places." Water, oak forests and mountains were considered to be "thin places," as were saints' birthplaces and sites of past miracles or extraordinary events.

The significance of "thin places" drew the Celtic Christians into frequent pilgrimages. Celts valued traveling for a spiritual purpose, to visit a place or places where God might be close by. In *Discovering Celtic Christianity*, Bruce Reed Pullen describes five characteristics of Celtic pilgrimages.[3] These principles apply to pilgrimages today.

1. "Pilgrimage is purposeful; it has a destination." Sometimes we undertake a pilgrimage to return to a place of memories; sometimes we go someplace new, where we anticipate a deeper connection with God. Wherever we go, we expect a significant, integrated connection between our inner journey of faith and this outer journey. The Celts undertook pilgrimages not because an abbot or priest suggested it, but because of an inner prompting. They undertook their journeys "for the love of Christ."[4]

2. "Pilgrimage is renewing." We might not know why we are drawn to a place, but we expect that our inner being will be renewed and revitalized because of what we experience.

3. "Pilgrimage is a time for reflection." A pilgrim may resemble a tourist for part of the day, looking at interesting sites and absorbing the historical aspects of a certain place. But a pilgrim always draws on Jesus' pattern of prayerful reflection, taking time to be alone with God as a part of the journey.

4. "When a pilgrimage includes other pilgrims, the excitement of the journey is shared." The Celtic experience of community spilled over to pilgrimages. Certainly some Celts went on pilgrimages alone, but others shared the experience with a partner or small group of fellow travelers.

5. "Pilgrimage transforms us." A pilgrimage is a journey taken in search of the holy, and the Celts understood that it is impossible to encounter our Holy God without being changed in some way—perhaps as expected or, more likely, in an very unexpected way. In fact, the very nature of a pilgrimage enables us to expect the unexpected. Pilgrims give up their commitment to planning and control, and they allow God to lead and guide.

Many people at midlife will feel an immediate connection with the Celtic Christians' sense of place, their understanding of "thin places" and their love of pilgrimage. At midlife, many become more aware of God's presence breaking through into everyday life. In brief moments of insight, we experience the supernatural touching the physical world. It feels wonderful to know that someone somewhere gave a name to this experience.

At midlife, we may begin to understand more deeply our connection with the places in our lives. Kathleen Norris's book *Dakota: A Spiritual Geography* expresses her connection with South Dakota. Her thoughts helped me understand how profoundly I am rooted in

---

The Pilgrim Searches for the Holy

A "pilgrim" is one who dedicates a period of time to the search for the holy, for a closer experience of the living God. The pilgrim travels light and wears comfortable clothing. Serious pilgrims combine both the outward journey toward a holy place and the inward journey toward self-understanding. Humor and laughter help to make the journey enjoyable when both frustration and fun, rain and rainbows, and stark scenery and beautiful horizons are encountered along with way. Worship, both private and public, is often part of the journey. A pilgrim is patient, knowing that eventually the journey will end in arrival, and in that arriving will be blessings as never before.

BRUCE REED PULLEN, *Discovering Celtic Christianity*

---

the Pacific Northwest and how closely, in my experience, God is connected with the water and mountains and trees that I see all the time.

Pilgrimages take on increased meaning at midlife. We may take a pilgrimage to a place of significance from our childhood or from our parents' lives. How many Americans at midlife or beyond have visited the Normandy beaches and the Nazi concentration camps with a sense of pilgrimage?

I recently visited the town in Virginia where I lived in junior high. We left Virginia when I was 14, and I had never been back. We found the houses I lived in, the schools I attended, the church where I went to Sunday school, and the beach and pool where I swam. My husband said he had never seen me so happy. I didn't set out to find these places with a spirit of pilgrimage, but as I look back on that visit, I definitely feel that I found something holy, a piece of my childhood stamped with the presence of God in those formative years of my life.

I take a group of women from our church to a monastery in Idaho every year, and that journey feels like a pilgrimage. As we drive across the eastern part of Washington State, a broad, wind-tossed landscape, we feel the stresses and irritations of city life dropping away. The trip prepares us for the profound silence and warm hospitality we find at the monastery, which enable us to look at our lives afresh with God's eyes.

The Celts were not people full of plans, organization and the need to control. They expected God's guidance on each step of their pilgrimage journeys, and they had an amazing ability to expect God to work through the events of daily life. As I undertake pilgrimages, where I give up some degree of control, I can feel myself practicing the kind of responsiveness they had toward God.

The Earth and Art

It's no accident that there are rabbits, mice, lizards and fish drawn between the lines and around the edges of the pages of the Book of Kells. The profound connection that the Celts felt between their lives and God's creation spilled over into their art.

Sister John Miriam Jones, in her book *With an Eagle's Eye*, writes that their sense of God's presence and love led the Celts "to artistic expressions using metal, wood, stone, paint, words, and music. These wholehearted artlovers found countless ways to utilize art in expressing their beliefs and their love. The monastic era coincides with the production of the best of Celtic metalwork, manuscripts and sculpture—all of which attest to their awareness of and yearning for God's immanent presence." She believes that all this creativity and artistry come from the truth that "deeply felt love requires expression."[5]

The Celts saw in the creation the deep love of the Creator, and they felt moved to create also. Their art was deeply symbolic. The Celtic knots that have become so popular in jewelry and art are symbolic of the love of God, which has no beginning or end.

The Celtic cross, which has also become popular in recent years, is a cross with a circle behind it. The circle probably represents the earth or the sun, and the cross represents Jesus dying to conquer the forces of evil. To the Celts, the cross as a shape in art would never be separated from the strong meaning of Jesus' death.

Many of the ancient high crosses in Ireland and Britain, large stone works of art with a worn frieze decorating the surface of each

---

Integration of So Many Things

"My background was Roman Catholic and Assembly of God, and I didn't know how to marry them. I would go into Bible studies in my Assembly of God church and say, 'We should take care of the environment,' and no one would respond. On every subject, I got lots of answers, but no questions, no mystery. Among Catholics, I would talk about the importance of an active faith that relies on the Holy Spirit, and no one could relate. In both settings, I saw in church life a dichotomy between the physical world and the spiritual world. The Celtic Christians just did not see that split. I found in Celtic Christianity an integration of so many things: care for creation, reliance on the Holy Spirit, the presence of God in everyday life, God being present and real yet also full of mystery. I get so frustrated that we have lost so much of the unique and balanced Celtic world view."

SANDRA, *age 30*

---

cross, show the story of our God who rescues, saves and feeds us. Often both the crucified Christ and the risen Christ are depicted. On many of the crosses Christ is shown with outstretched, wounded hands to bless the world as both Creator and Redeemer.

Part of the appeal of Celtic Christianity at midlife is this connection between the creation, artistic expression and our faith in God. As we experience God's handiwork in nature in a more profound way, we may identify with the Celts who lived among the trees and hills and woodland animals and who saw all of nature as an expression of God's creativity and as a true gift from God.

As we find new artistic expression at midlife, whether it's quilting or drawing or baking or making music or woodworking or writing poetry, we can receive deep encouragement and challenge from the Celts, who seamlessly integrated their faith with their art. They created art for the love of Christ. They experienced themselves as connected to their Creator as they pursued artistic expression, and they expressed their understanding of God in symbols that were full of meaning for them. We can do the same.

These symbols and images take on increased importance at midlife, when we long to break free of the pervasive, materialistic images bombarding us in the media and to deepen our connection to the eternal and the holy. Celtic knots and scampering mice can become anchors for us, connecting us to God in a nonverbal but profound way. Esther de Waal, herself descended from Celts, writes in her wonderful book *The Celtic Way of Prayer*:

> Above all the Celtic tradition has reminded me of the importance of images, those foundational images whose depths and universal character have always brought such riches to Christian understanding. Most people today are being constantly battered by the succession of superficial images that meet us in the world of consumerism, in television and in advertising, where there is no chance to spend time testing their true meaning. Therefore, it now becomes vital, more than ever, to recover the fundamental images of fire, wind, bread, water, of light and dark, of the heart. These are the great impersonal symbols that are universal, understood by Christian and non-Christian alike. An Indian Christian priest once said that they were like a great bridge that Christ has thrown across the world and across history so that men and women may walk to meet each other and be completed in him.[6]

The Trinity

Deeply ingrained in the heart and soul of Celtic Christian spirituality is the mystery of one God in three persons, a truth that is taught clearly in the Bible, even though the word *Trinity* is not found in Scripture. Three in one; one in three. Esther de Waal writes:

> Here is a profound experience of God from a people who are deeply Trinitarian without any philosophical struggle about how that is to be expressed intellectually. Perhaps the legend of St. Patrick stooping down to pick up the shamrock in order to explain the Trinity is after all more significant than we might have thought. It is as though he were saying to those early Irish people: Your God is a God who is Three-in-One and this is the most natural and immediately accessible thing in the world.[7]

The image of three in one is found frequently in Celtic art and poetry. Analogies from nature and daily life permeate the Celtic poems about the Trinity:

> Three folds of the cloth, yet only one napkin is there,
> Three joints in the finger, but still only one figure fair,
> Three leaves of the shamrock, yet no more than one
>   shamrock to wear,
> Frost, snow-flakes and ice, all in water their origin share,
> Three Persons in God; to one God alone we make prayer.[8]

Sometimes Celtic poems go on at length about the Holy Three, but some are brief and vivid, like this one:

> O Father who sought me
> O Son who bought me
> O Holy Spirit who taught me.[9]

I wonder if enthusiasm for the Trinity has fallen into disfavor because our generation has such a high need to be able to explain and understand everything in a rational way. I can remember as a child being very enthusiastic about the Trinity. In my simple childhood faith, I enjoyed the riddle of one being three and three being one. The Celts' enthusiasm for this great mystery has rekindled in me a joy and wonder at the great truth that we simply cannot understand everything about God, and we don't need to.

Community

Celtic culture was monastic and communal. Villages centered around small monasteries, and the prayer and devotion of the monks contagiously spread into village life. Ordinary village people often prayed the daily offices—the liturgical daily prayers at set times—with the monks or at home with their families. The pattern of each day was punctuated with calls to prayer at specific times. This created a rhythm in each day and a rhythm over the course of the year as the prayers changed to reflect the church calendar.

The Celts embraced community in part because they were so aware of their connection to angels and saints. The Celts' "thin places" reflected their awareness of the ways the supernatural realm touches the physical realm; the angels and saints, to the Celts, were close by at certain times and in certain places. This gave them a sense of community with the angels and saints, and that sense of community spilled over into community with the people around them.

The Celts looked for people to act as mentors for them, and they called those mentors "soul friends." Having a soul friend was an integral part of living in community. In our day, more people are finding great help from working with a spiritual director, a person to meet with on a regular schedule, perhaps monthly, who helps us discern the hand of God in our lives. Soul friends fulfilled that same role, but often the relationship went both ways in an equal partnership. This tradition of deep friendships centered in Christ can feel very attractive at midlife, as we desire to intentionally draw nearer to God. A partner on the journey feels like a helpful support.

Women were valued as leaders in Celtic Christian society, and the female leaders of monasteries for women were regarded with as much respect as the male leaders of monasteries. Brigid of Kildare and Hilda of Whitby are just two examples of women who founded monasteries and were viewed as leaders in the wider Christian community.[10] The leadership of women, along with the partnership between men and women, was one of the aspects of Christian community that was lost when the church in the Celtic lands became more connected to the Roman church.

Celtic Christians embraced the importance of hospitality, aware that the way they treated strangers mirrored the way they treated Christ. According to Sister John Miriam Jones, they "treasured the sacramental understanding, 'Christ in friend and stranger.' "[11] The Celts exercised hospitality as a community.

Celtic Christians also valued mission very highly. Sister Jones writes, "Celtic monks had a compulsion to share the joy of their consciousness of the Holy Three and of God's creation. The gospel dictum of mission allowed such sharing, and they seemed possessed by that call. . . . Within their passionate style of evangelization was a sensitivity to the human dignity of those they encountered. . . . They respected the responses of those who resisted. Ultimately missionary efforts were viewed as the Holy Spirit's domain, so despite the intensity of their work, the results were accepted with humility and abandonment."[12] Mission was viewed as the calling of the community, and mission efforts were undertaken by the community.

Another aspect of Celtic Christian community, which may seem unusual to us, is their embrace of silence. Silence was an important discipline in the Celtic monastic tradition, and that tradition influenced everyday life outside the monasteries. We may find it easy to believe that community always involves a lot of communication; the Celts embraced silence as a form of communication with God that forms one of the foundations for community life.

At midlife, this blending of silence and community can sound more attractive than earlier in life. Time to think and pray, time to reflect, becomes more important for many. The security of the embrace of the community, to uphold us and encourage us as we reflect, think and pray, feels like a wonderful balance.

The Celts' practice of their faith was so integrated and wholistic. Hospitality, mission, art, connection to the earth, men and women serving together, silence and community were all woven together as a seamless garment. Their unified faith that spread into every aspect of life can be a tremendous model for us as we seek to live in relationship with God within our fragmented culture.

Celtic Christian Prayer

> I am giving Thee love with my whole devotion,
> I am giving Thee kneeling with my whole desire,
> I am giving Thee love with my whole heart. . . .
> I am giving Thee my soul, O God of all Gods.[13]

Celtic Christian prayer is full of praise and thankfulness, devotion and commitment, and deep sorrow for sin. The prayers and songs in *Carmina Gadelica* draw us into a kind of prayer that involves the whole self: mind, body and soul.

The call to prayer, so strong in Celtic Christianity, finds it roots in the strong sense of the Triune God: God the Father who created us, God the Son who redeemed us, and God the Spirit who indwells us. This is not a vague kind of prayer to the universe or to an unknown God. We may find it easy to think that because the Celts loved nature so much and found God so visible in his creation, they directed their prayers to that creation. Not at all. It is God revealed in Christ through the power of the Spirit who called them to prayer and to whom they directed their prayers.

Prayer with the Whole of Myself

I have come to see that the Celtic way of prayer is prayer with the whole of myself, a totality of praying that embraces the fullness of my own personhood, and allows me not only to pray with words but also, more important, with the heart, the feelings, using image and symbol, touching the springs of my imagination.

ESTHER DE WAAL, *The Celtic Way of Prayer*

The Celts desired to praise God with their whole beings. "My speech—may it praise you without flaw; may my heart love you, King of Heaven and of earth."[14] Another poem says:

> Lord, be it thine,
> > Unfaltering praise of mine!
> To thee my whole heart's love be given
> > Of earth and Heaven Thou King divine![15]

The Celtic poems and prayers express deep gratitude for the created world, for the beauty of doe and fawn and horse, flowers in bloom, purple heather, the honeybees, the fish in the swift streams, even the grains of sand and the clods of earth. The prayers move smoothly from thankfulness for the beauty of the earth to praise for the God of glory, the Trinity, the loving Father, the redeeming Son.

The Celts help to bring us back to an Old Testament sense of thankfulness based on the acts of God—on what God has done for all of us, not just for me. Celtic prayers focused more on thankfulness than on asking God to give them something:

> Each thing I have received from Thee it came,
> > Each thing for which I hope, from Thy love it will come,
> Each thing I enjoy, it is of Thy bounty,
> > Each thing I ask, comes of Thy disposing.[16]

The Celtic Christian emphasis on thankfulness rather than petition can be a helpful teacher on the midlife journey. In our materialistic and acquisitive culture, where we are told over and over again that we don't have enough and that more is always better, we need to stop listening to the insistent voices of the media and focus very simply on what God has already given us. First and foremost, God has given us his presence in all of life. God has given us forgiveness through Jesus Christ, a beautiful world to live in, and friends and family around us. We find it hard to notice our blessings because we focus so strongly on what we don't have. The Celts remind us that the discipline of thankfulness will enable us to see the riches of the world God has given us.

Celtic Christians had a strong sense of evil in the world, with a particularly keen sense of their own tendency toward evil. This influenced their patterns of prayer in a profound way, calling them to express sorrow and sadness in prayer as well as joy and thankfulness. They understood clearly that the death of Jesus was absolutely necessary to buy back the universe from Satan, who had taken the world under his power because of human sin. Again, because of the Celts' joy in nature, it would be easy to believe that they saw everything as good. Instead, they had a healthy balance between the wonder of the created world and the presence of evil in that world. With world events in our day showing us evil in new ways and inciting fear for our personal and national future, it's especially important that we achieve a balance like that of the Celts.

Esther de Waal writes about the sense of guilt that bedeviled her childhood, the sense of never being good enough, of failing again and again in trying to measure up. In the Celts there is none of that kind of self-focused guilt. Instead, she notes that in the Celtic poems and songs "I have found sorrow, deep sorrow, many tears, a real outpouring of grief, but it is never turned in on itself, never the kind of sorrow that becomes inward, self-destructive guilt, feeding on itself. Tears, as I learn them from the Celtic Christian tradition, are never what so often my own tears become: tears of rage or of self-pity, tears of frustration, tears because I have put my own self at the center of the picture and feel that I have not received the treatment that I deserve—the tears of a child, in fact, for whom 'life isn't fair.'. . . But true tears are those of real, deep personal sorrow, of repentance, that lead to the determination to change."[17]

Bathing the Day in Prayer

My travels to Ireland have changed me, most noticeably in my desire to infuse my own life with more quiet. Celtic spirituality embraces the necessity for silence and solitude in order to connect with God, to hear him, to renew one's self. The lush Irish countryside invites this kind of tranquility, but I have found that intentional quiet moments can be equally fulfilling right in my own living room in the middle of fast-paced America.

The Celtic view of prayer is simple and comprehensive: pray all the time. The Apostle Paul's command, "Be joyful always, pray continually; give thanks in all circumstances" (1 Thessalonians 5:16-18), is taken quite literally. There are volumes of books written on Celtic prayer that include prayers for every action that might occur in a normal day. From waking to eating to working to playing to sleeping, Celtic spirituality bathes each day in prayer.

LOIS RABEY, *"Celtic Christianity"* <www.womenoffaith.com>

The Celtic Christian patterns of prayer are very appropriate as a part of the midlife journey. We may find ourselves longing for an authentic spiritual practice involving the whole self. Celtic Christian prayer isn't a superficial practice involving only a part of life. The Celts brought themselves, their very beings, to God in gratitude, in praise and in sorrow.

The Paradoxes in Celtic Christianity

At midlife, many of us are drawn to integrate the various parts of our life. The Celtic worldview was beautifully integrated, with all aspects of life a part of a greater whole. This integration was possible because the Celts were comfortable with paradox and mystery. The awareness of mystery grows stronger for many at midlife, and we can learn from the Celts.

Some of the paradoxes embraced by the Celtic Christians are:

◆ God is present in nature and in everyday life through his Spirit, yet God is also the exalted Creator and Redeemer. God is in all but also above all—both immanent and transcendent.

◆ God is one God, yet God is three persons in community with one another.

◆ We can experience God through our emotions, and we can also experience God through our minds.

◆ God is at home with us in our daily life, yet God also calls us to pilgrimages where we will learn new things about him and experience him in new ways.

◆ Nature is good, it is beautiful, and it displays the artistry of the Creator, yet evil is present in nature and in human nature.

◆ The spiritual realm is close by and frequently touches our physical world, yet the spiritual realm is most fulfilled in heaven, which is a totally separate place.

◆ God gives us great and wonderful blessings, and God is present when we experience good things, yet God is also present through our sufferings, which teach us and shape us.

Anyone who has lived a few years of life has experienced some of the paradoxes of life. The Celtic Christian acceptance of paradox without the need to explain everything can bring a wonderful perspective of lightness and joy at midlife.

Ross's Story

Ross, 62, is a retired businessman who has been studying Celtic Christianity for many years. His involvement in creating an illuminated biblical passage in the Celtic style has helped him enter into the values and integrated worldview of the Celts.

* * *

Celtic Christianity allowed God to reach me on all sorts of levels. The Book of Kells and the other Celtic illuminated manuscripts made me see another side of God's truth, the way truth is connected with beauty.

I am awed by the Celtic monks' willingness to put their lives into their art. I am awed by the beauty, elegance and style of their art. Those dear brothers and sisters prepared themselves for the holy task of working with Scripture. Before they picked up a brush each day, they spent time in confession and received forgiveness. They viewed their work very much as a part of their worship.

I myself am working on a piece of Celtic art. I've got a nice big piece of vellum, and I've sketched out a Scripture verse. In this fast paced world, where you can generate a piece of computer art in a few minutes, it's amazing to think of the time and effort lavished on each page of the Book of Kells. Working on my own Celtic art connects me with the patience and long vision of the Celtic monks. It may take me ten years to have something of quality that can be passed on.

There's a lot to it. The art, the chemistry of mixing the colors, the challenge of working with gold leaf. The Celts were so integrated with God's creation, and I experience a little of that integration as I work on my own piece of art.

* * *

Questions for Reflection

To think about, write about or talk about with friends.

1. Where are the "thin places" in your life—times and places where God seems particularly present? Spend some time thanking God for those places. Reflect on what you could do to be in those places more often.

2. Pick one of the Celtic prayers in this chapter and copy it into your daily calendar or onto a slip of paper. Look at the poem several times a day and pray the words, in anticipation of a greater sense of God's presence with you throughout the day.

3. Which of the paradoxes embraced by Celtic Christians feels most comfortable to you? Which seems most uncomfortable? Why? Spend some time reflecting on and praying about the role of paradox in your life.

For Further Reading

Esther de Waal. *The Celtic Way of Prayer: The Recovery of the Religious Imagination.* New York: Doubleday, 1997.

John Miriam Jones, S.C. *With an Eagle's Eye: A Seven-Day Sojourn in Celtic Spirituality.* Notre Dame, Ind.: Ave Maria Press, 1998.

Bruce Reed Pullen. *Discovering Celtic Christianity.* Mystic, Conn.: Twenty-Third Publications, 1999.

4

Enjoying God's World
Worshiping the Creator

Wᵉ've seen in Celtic Christianity a strong affirmation of God as Creator. Celtic Christians experienced God's presence in groves of trees, in the light of the fire and in the changing seasons. God made all of those things, they believed, and God uses everything he has made to teach us about himself.

In this chapter we will explore further the role of God's creation in calling us to prayer, worship and simplicity. So many people at midlife have told me about the growing sense of awe and wonder they experience in nature. They feel connected to God through the beauty around them, through creative activities and through careful stewardship of creation. God the Creator feels closer and more real to many at midlife.

Ever since my college years I have had a strong sense of God speaking to me through nature, and my awareness of God's voice through creation has become even stronger in recent years. Nature seems more beautiful, and I need it more. I thought my life was complicated and challenging two decades ago! I am now juggling more balls than I could have imagined then. In the midst of the stress and complexity of daily life, I need a sense of God's eternity and peace more than I ever have before. It is often the beauty of nature that gives me the sense of timelessness and serenity I need. With the increasing violence and terror in our world, I need God as a refuge more than ever before. It is often creation that helps me find my security in God and then helps me stay rooted in God's transcendence, power and love.

In addition to my need for the serenity that so often comes from the creation, I have found that I am now experiencing the beauty of the out-of-doors more intensely than ever before. Right around my fortieth birthday, the spring flowers began to seem more abundant than in previous years. When I noticed this increased beauty, I thought the weather pattern was changing in some way to bring on more flowers. But other people said, "More flowers?" As the seasons flowed by and each spring seemed more beautiful than any spring before, I realized that the change was coming from inside *me*. Each year I seem to be growing in my ability to observe.

That increased ability to notice the details in nature is intimately connected with my awareness of God's presence in my life. I am full of awe that God would lavish such creativity on the variety of rhododendron flowers: the tiny spots on the petals, the subtle variations of color, the overall blast of color when observed from a distance. Surely if God cares so much about a plant, he must care for me. Surely if he has taken such care with the design of rhododendrons, he must care about the design of my life, and he must be shepherding me as I go about my daily life. The beauty of nature gives me great comfort because it speaks to me of the abundance of God's grace, outpoured in my life.

By the time midlife arrives, most of us have also experienced sadness at the way nature has been damaged by human carelessness and greed. This abundant earth that God created no longer feeds all its inhabitants because humans have selfishly divided up its riches in inequitable ways. Natural disasters and droughts have stunned us by their impact on people we care about.

For many, all the evil we have witnessed makes the beauty of creation even more precious. It is a mystery how our awe and wonder at God's creation can coexist with so much sadness because of the evil that pervades nature and human nature. Yet the creation keeps speaking to us, telling us how awesome God is.

Bill's Story

Bill, 35, is an urban planner who works for an architectural firm.

*   *   *

I am fundamentally at home in nature. I grew up spear-fishing for flounder with my dad, riding bikes a lot, hiking in the mountains with my Boy Scout troop. From an early age, looking at the stars, when I would let myself experience it fully, it felt overwhelming. You just can't take it all in.

I enjoy the seasons. I'm just starting to get a sense of age and cycle and process in my life, and seeing it in nature is comforting somehow.

There were a lot of difficult parts about my life growing up. I was sort of a mournful kid. Fall was my favorite season because it felt mournful, so I was comforted by fall. Fall helped me tune into my own nature.

As I've gotten older, the meaning of spring has become more real. I'm crazy about spring. I like the freshness, everything budding out. It's exciting to me, and it connects me to my emotions somehow, where it didn't in the past.

I've started gardening. I love the rhythm of it, seeing stuff come out of the garden. It's a non-verbal thing, a connection with nature. It's ordinary and yet not ordinary.

Nature has always been pretty important to me, but I'm experiencing it now in a way that's somehow more present. In gardening, the sense of planning, designing, bringing it along—there's something very rooted about that. It's not directly about God, but it feels like I'm tuning in with spirituality and my home and where I live.

The universe is huge. I see God in the hugeness. Our smallness is both spatial and temporal—we're such a small piece of the puzzle.

The creation also speaks to me about the co-creativity of humanity. We're created in God's image and God fundamentally is creative. In many ways, that's an exciting frontier of faith for me. Creativity is a huge gift to us. You can see God's creativity in people, but one of the most accessible ways to experience God's creativity is in creation.

I'm an urban planner, and I've loved maps all my life. Now I'm thinking about what goes onto maps. My firm is designing a large project, and I'm thinking about the wetlands and the topography, how best to develop it. How do we turn this landscape into a place for humans in a way that is respectful of the way God made it?

Urban design ties into environmental policy and the political process in caring for God's creation, trying to be responsive to God's creativity. It's such a profound change in how we look at the world. So many pieces can come into play as we try to care for the environment. We Christians have focused our theology and our attention on humans and on God. We haven't taken the creation into account as we should have.

* * *

Nature Calls Us to Worship God

A few years ago I was talking with a friend from childhood. I asked her about her sense of faith, and she said that she was basically a druid. I asked her what she meant, and she replied that she experiences God in nature. For her, nature enables her to experience a sense of transcendence, and nature is her church. Any worship she experiences is in nature.

I said to her, "I can really relate to that. I often experience God in nature."

She replied, "Wait a minute. You're a Christian. How can you say that?"

I answered, "God created everything. When I look at the world he made, I see it as his handiwork. We can learn something about artists from looking at their artwork, and, in the same way, we can experience something of God in nature. That doesn't mean nature equals God. It just means it reveals something about God because he made it and sustains it. Because nature is so beautiful, it speaks to me of God's beauty."

The Earth Is Full of God's Glory

The Spirit of the LORD *has made me,*
and the breath of the Almighty gives me life. (Job 33:4)
Holy, holy, holy is the Lord of hosts;
the whole earth is full of his glory. (Is 6:3)
I brought you into a plentiful land
to eat its fruits and its good things.
But when you entered you defiled my land,
and made my heritage an abomination. (Jer 2:7)

Christians have often been wary of talking too much about finding God in nature because they might sound like pantheists instead of Christians. Pantheism asserts that God is everywhere; in fact, to a pantheist the universe in its totality is God. Christians believe that God made and sustains the physical world, and God is present everywhere through his Spirit, but God is also separate from creation, just as artists are separate from the artwork they create.

Pastor and writer Gordon MacDonald describes the way his grandmother helped him learn to enjoy birds, trees, animals and plants, teaching him that "the things we were seeing were God's gift, God's expression of his character, and God's artistry." He writes:

> As I became more acquainted with theology, I began to realize that Grandmother had been teaching me one of the most fundamental truths of the Bible: God had created something out of nothing. That creation reflected a signal part of his nature: order, beauty, energy, growth. I saw that the world was a vast sanctuary where one, stimulated by his or her senses, could be caused to worship and behold a primary revelation of God the Creator.[1]

Many people at midlife experience in a new way the physical world as a sanctuary that enables us to praise and worship God.

This is not a new idea, yet it is an idea that has been largely lost in the twentieth-century church. Over and over again, the psalm writers are moved to adoration and worship because of the splendor of nature. Psalm 33:1-9 calls us to "rejoice in the LORD" and "sing to him a new song" for several reasons: his word is upright, he loves righteousness and justice, and he made the earth. "Let all the earth fear the LORD . . . for he spoke and it came to be" (Ps 33:8-9).

The whole creation belongs to God by virtue of the fact that he made it. "The earth is the LORD's and all that is in it, the world, and those who live in it; for he has founded it on the seas, and established it on the rivers" (Ps 24:1-2). Everything about it belongs to him: the animals and plants, the stars and planets, even the rhythms of nature. "Yours is the day, yours also is the night . . . you made summer and winter" (Ps 74:16-17).

The creation helps me put my own life into perspective. "Long ago you laid the foundation of the earth, and the heavens are the work of your hands. They will perish, but you endure" (Ps 102:25-26). My own life on earth will end. All the beauty of nature is temporal. Nature itself is definitely not God, because nature will ultimately perish. Only God is eternal.

The way that God sustains the physical world is a call to praise and thankfulness.

> Sing to the LORD with thanksgiving,
>> make melody to our God on the lyre.
> He covers the heavens with clouds,
>> prepares rain for the earth,
>> makes grass grow on the hills.
> He gives to the animals their food,
>> and to the young ravens when they cry. (Ps 147:7-9)

We are called to praise God, as is the whole creation. "Praise him, sun and moon; praise him, all you shining stars! . . . Let them praise the name of the LORD, for he commanded and they were created" (Ps 148:3, 5).

Psalm 104 is the most extensive piece of biblical literature that focuses on God as Creator and Sustainer of the universe. John Stott calls it "perhaps the earliest essay in ecology in the literature of the world."[2] It opens with the words:

> Bless the LORD, O my soul.
>> O LORD my God, you are very great.
> You are clothed with honor and majesty,
>> wrapped in light as with a garment.
> You stretch out the heavens like a tent,
>> you set the beams of your chambers on the waters. (Ps 104:1-3)

The psalm goes on to describe the way God created the earth and the way he sustains it with water and food. The language is amazingly concrete: springs gush forth, grass grows for cattle. Specific animals and plants are mentioned: cedars, storks, young lions, wild goats. The psalmist says all the plants and animals look to God for food in their season. In fact, it is God who takes away the breath of animals when they die, and it is God who gives the breath that enables them to live.

After thirty verses describing God's hand in nature, the psalmist bursts out, "May the glory of the LORD endure forever," then continues, "I will sing to the LORD as long as I live; I will sing praise to my God while I have being" (vv. 31, 33).

Psalm 104 seems to be a partner to Psalm 103, which focuses on God as Redeemer. Psalms 103 and 104, taken together, give a picture of the God of relationship who redeems and heals human beings and calls them into relationship with him, who is the same God who created and sustains the physical universe. Often the psalms flow seamlessly from praising God as Creator to praising God for his compassion, his justice, his righteousness.

Throughout the psalms, there is a pattern of God's revelation both in nature and in his word. Psalm 19 says, "The heavens are telling the glory of God" (v. 1). Later in the same psalm, in verses 7-10, the psalmist describes the wonders of the law of the Lord, the written revelation of God. God has made himself known to us through the creation—and also through his special communication with humans in the Bible and in his Son, Jesus Christ. Nature alone cannot teach us all we need to know about God. Yet when we neglect seeing God's hand in nature, we miss a powerful call to worship and a deep connection with the humility that comes from knowing we are created beings dependent on our Creator God.

The Work of His Hands

I've listed a lot of Scriptures that describe God's voice in nature because of my own personal journey in this area. For a long time I didn't know those Scriptures were there, and I thought my love for God's creation and my experience of his presence in nature were unique to me.

I majored in biology, and some of my most intense worship experiences occurred in biology lab looking through a microscope at algae's glowing green complex structures. For my last two years of college, I worked as a lab assistant for an astronomy professor, and I loved learning about the vastness of interstellar space. The hugeness of the universe and the smallness of bacteria spoke to me of the greatness of our Creator God. The strange and beautiful shapes of lichens and the awesome silence of the stars gave me a perspective on my life and an awareness of God's majesty that I couldn't find elsewhere.

God seemed so real to me in his handiwork, the created world, but no one else seemed to be having the same experience. In college in the 1970s, no one that I ran into was talking or writing about God and nature. Yet my sense of God's voice in nature was so real to me. In my good moments, I thought I had discovered a source of food for my soul that was unique to me. (In my bad moments, I thought I was out of my mind, that I was bordering on heresy of some kind.)

Slowly but surely, since then, God has brought my attention to the Scriptures I have listed in detail for you. Articles and books have been published that focus on a biblical view of creation. I have listed some of them at the end of this chapter, and I will quote from them throughout the chapter. I have come to understand that it is totally natural and right that creation would speak to me of God's character and his love. I wasn't out of my mind at all when I experienced the creation as one of my teachers about God's character. In fact, God ordained that the work of his hands would call us to prayer and praise. Enjoying the creation with God can be an integral part of growing into a deeper relationship with him.

I am concerned that this emphasis is too often missing from our Christian life today. We are good at acknowledging God as our Redeemer, the righteous one who communicates to us through the Bible and calls us into relationship through his Son, Jesus. Yet we have neglected to see God's handiwork in nature as a call to prayer and praise. We have missed something central to the Old Testament understanding of who God is and how God communicates.

Maybe this omission comes from our fear that we will be viewed as pantheists if we talk about God's hand in creation. Maybe the pervasive emphasis of New Age thinking has made us fearful that we will

---

Praising God in Partnership with Creation

"I live near a lake. It's two and a half miles around the lake. I walk it, I run around it. There's an old fir grove around the lake a ways from my house. The trees stand really straight and beautiful. One day when I was walking by, I felt a presence. I felt it beckon to me, but I was afraid. I started to cry. Later I began to notice something happening to me when I'd get to that place. Once I heard a voice, "You must be empty to be filled." Once I gained an insight about light and dark.

"I've named the place 'The Brotherwood.' The brown bark makes the trees look like monks. It's a holy place, a place I pray and am quiet, waiting to hear. I bring concerns there. If I'm sad, it's the first place I go. If I'm happy, I go there. Those trees are my praying community. As I run around the lake, I see the trees praising God, their branches lifted up.

"People talk about the energy in cathedrals. I do believe there are holy places, and I stumbled onto one. Or maybe my heart was open and I was ready."

PENNY, *age 39*

---

lose a biblical perspective if we think too highly of creation. The New Testament doesn't talk as much about God the Creator as the psalms do, and maybe we are concerned that we need to faithfully reflect the priorities of the New Testament. Maybe we like viewing ourselves as autonomous human beings who don't need to depend on God for every breath and every meal. I don't know for sure what has caused the focus on God the Redeemer while neglecting God the Creator, but I do know that we are missing something wonderful.

Many folks rediscover the joys of worshiping God the Creator through something as simple as smelling roses or enjoying the feel of the wind on their face. Whatever form it takes, our fresh sense of the Lord is consistent with the joy and wonder that the psalm writers experienced when they considered the wonders of creation.

The Good Creation

At the end of each day of creation, God looked at what he had made and declared it "good." The description of creation in the first two chapters of Genesis is one of the most beautiful pieces of literature ever written, emphasizing God's power to create and the wonder and beauty of his work in creation.

Ron Sider writes that, according to the Bible,

> the material world is so good that the one who created all things and pronounced them very good actually became flesh. The material world is so good that Jesus rose bodily from the tomb. The material world is so good that all believers will be resurrected bodily to dance and revel in a renewed creation when the Lord returns. That's how good the material world is. Consequently, God wants you and me to rejoice now in the good earth's bounty.[3]

Sider goes on to call us to a passionate commitment to Jesus Christ that manifests the truth that nothing in life is more important than our love of Jesus. This kind of love, he believes, will result in care for the poor as well as care for the environment.

Soon after God created humans, he gave them the task of "tilling and tending" the garden (Gen 2:15). For those of us who live in an urban setting, it may be hard to imagine what those commands imply for us. At times I have grown vegetables in my back yard. Is that what is meant by God's command to "till and tend" the garden?

Calvin DeWitt, a theologian and professor of environmental studies, points out the range of meaning of these words. The Hebrew word translated "till" can also mean dress, work or serve. The word translated "tend" can also be translated as keep, take care of, guard or look after. The root word that lies behind "tend" indicates a loving, caring, sustaining kind of keeping.

DeWitt asks, "How on earth can we serve creation? Shouldn't creation serve us instead?"[4]

DeWitt, like Ronald Sider, believes that the first call is to be a disciple of Jesus Christ, and out of that discipleship will come concern for

---

Our Earthly Home

So we see, then, these four great truths in the Bible concerning our earthly home:

1. *The earth is good, not bad.*
2. *The earth is diseased and disordered because of sin.*
3. *The earth is our responsibility as God's stewards.*
4. *The earth will be judged and restored.*

How should this make a difference in the way we, as Christians, live?

1. *We may enjoy God's good creation and praise God for it.*
2. *We may live before the world as good stewards of the earth. Christians should be at the forefront of modeling good stewardship principles, including care of creation. Minimally, this certainly includes recycling, healthy eating, and supporting sound environmental policies in government and business.*
3. *We may honor and support those Christians whom God calls to a ministry to the earth.*
4. *We can teach and model earth stewardship to our children.*
5. *We can continue to study Scripture to learn what it says about the earth. For too long, many vital texts have been overlooked by the church. We can correct this blind spot by searching out God's vision for the earth.*

HOWARD SNYDER, *"This World Is Not My Home?"* The Best Preaching on Earth

---

the care and sustaining of creation. Serving and taking care of the garden, which he takes to mean the whole created world, will mean careful use of resources, striving to find our contentment in God rather than in things, and enjoyment of creation without destroying it. DeWitt also argues that, as a part of caring for creation, we need to give animals and plants the kind of Sabbath rest that is prescribed in the Old Testament. All of this is necessary because of the human propensity to use things up, rather than use things carefully in a way that protects the earth for future generations.

In Romans 8 the apostle Paul talks about the fact that the whole creation was subjected to futility because of human sin. In fact, Paul writes, the creation itself groans, just as we do, waiting for the time of final redemption. The earth is not in its normal state, the way God created it. Human sin has marred human life; it has also had a disastrous impact on the creation.

In Hosea 4:1-3, the prophet describes human sin: faithlessness, lack of loyalty, lying, cursing, stealing, murder, adultery and bloodshed. Because of this, Hosea says, "The land mourns, and all who live in it languish; together with the wild animals and the birds of the air, even the fish of the sea are perishing." This passage could have been written today!

Howard Snyder writes that the biblical picture is not just a story of God and his people. "It is the story of God, the people, and the land. . . . Thus the Bible shows us that mistreating the earth is one of the clearest evidences of human sinfulness. We continue to sin against the earth—God's creation—when we pollute the earth, waste the earth's resources, or fail to practice good stewardship of the land entrusted to our care."[5]

Many at midlife feel increased concern about the environmental degradation all around us. As the preciousness of God's good creation becomes more real and more vivid, we realize the fragility of the beautiful earth. Many become more motivated to work for the protection of the environment as a part of their Christian commitment.

The love of nature that I began to experience in college nurtured in me a deep conviction that it is important to care for the earth. When I graduated from college in the mid-seventies, no one else seemed to share that belief. I have been delighted in recent years to watch an increasing commitment among Christians to care for the environment. A Christian college in Seattle sponsors a seminar for freshmen on Christians and the environment. Many of the quotations in this chapter come from a book of sermons on caring for creation, *The Best Preaching on Earth: Sermons on Caring for Creation.* Another book, *Cherish the Gift: A Congregational Guide to Earth Stewardship* by Cindy Ubben Causey, provides practical suggestions for Christian congregations that would like to be more faithful in their stewardship of the earth. All of these are signs to me that Christians are increasingly engaged in the issues of caring for the earth.

Worshiping the God of Materialistic Consumerism

You and I have a problem—in fact three problems. The environmental crisis is not a silly fiction created by mad scientists and political demagogues. There are dangerous holes in the ozone layer. Our waters, soil and air are polluted. . . . But we have a second problem. Some of the people most concerned about the ecological dangers tell us that historic Christianity is the problem. We must, they tell us, reject the biblical teaching that the Creator is distinct from the earth and that people alone are made in the image of God. . . . Australian scientist Pete Singer says that people are no more important than monkeys and mosquitoes. To think that we are more important is "speciesism." Fortunately, biblical Christians reject this theological nonsense. But then so often we turn around and worship the earth in a different way. By the cars we drive, the houses we purchase, the affluent lifestyles we live, we show that we really worship the god of materialistic consumerism. That's our third problem.

RON SIDER, *"Tending the Garden Without Worshipping It,"* The Best Preaching on Earth

---

This movement toward creation stewardship by Christians coincides nicely with midlife for baby boomers and older Gen-Xers, with so many of us experiencing an increased awareness of the wonder of creation. As we slow down to experience the joy of this moment in this particular place in God's creation, we understand more deeply

God's call to be careful stewards of all that God made. Part of that stewardship needs to be a reevaluation of the way we live in our consumer society.

Voluntary Simplicity

Day and night the beauty of nature speaks to us of God's greatness and calls us to praise and prayer. Day and night our consumer culture is also speaking to us, but the message is very different.

"More is better." "If you are feeling sad, discouraged or sexually unattractive, you will feel much, much better if you buy something." "Shop 'til you drop." These messages are pervasive in ads, TV sitcoms and talk shows, movies, magazines, newspapers and shop displays.

Our consumer culture seriously gets in the way of faithful stewardship of creation in a variety of ways. Possessions cost money, and many of us have to work harder to pay for our many things. The extra time spent working makes us hurried and scattered, much less able to be intentional about the way we live. Possessions have to be shopped for, maintained, repaired and housed, which requires time and effort that might have been spent doing something more restful and spiritually restoring. Everything we buy had to be made somewhere and then transported to us. The factories that make things and the trucks that transport things are often major polluters.

Richard Foster is very blunt in describing the seriousness of the consumer messages from our culture: "Our need for security has led us into an insane attachment to things. We really must understand that the lust for affluence in contemporary society is psychotic. It is psychotic because it has completely lost touch with reality. We crave things we neither need nor enjoy." Foster believes we get sucked into consumerism because "we lack a divine Center."[6]

One Christian response to consumerism is voluntary simplicity, choosing to live below the level of affluence that we can afford, in order to slow down consumption, live more intentionally and be more connected to what God desires for us. Many people who choose voluntary simplicity have a strong commitment to honoring God as Creator, because living more simply serves both the earth and the poor of the world. Voluntary simplicity has a particular appeal at midlife as we desire to strip away the extraneous possessions, commitments and values in our lives and embrace what really matters to us.

Voluntary simplicity is not another "should" or "ought." People who practice simplicity express enthusiasm for the joy they have experienced in embracing a different set of values than the ones promoted by our culture. They talk about the beauty in the words "less can be more." To understand the joy of simplicity, think for a moment about the difference between a huge bouquet of flowers and a single rose. Sometimes the huge bouquet is appropriate, but sometimes the single rose is the best option because its exquisite beauty is not obscured by a lot of other flowers.

Our culture tells us that huge bouquets are always best. We live, in effect, so surrounded by huge bouquets that we are overwhelmed by them. Simplicity offers a kind of beauty that is spare, clean, pure and straightforward.

Last year we offered a class at our church on the book *Rich Christians in an Age of Hunger* by Ronald Sider. In the 1997 revision of the book, Sider makes many connections between world poverty and environmental degradation, because it is usually the poor who suffer the most ill effects from the impact of pollution. About six months after the class, one woman in her forties who had attended told me about the great impact the class had on her.

Before reading the book, she had had no idea of the extent of world poverty or its connection to pollution. After the class, she prayed a lot about how to respond. God led her very clearly to start taking the bus to work two days a week instead of driving. She figured out that by taking the bus she is saving 2,500 miles a year of wear and tear on her car, which reduces both pollution and the carbon emissions that cause global warming. She has to change buses in downtown Seattle, and she finds that she often buys birthday cards and other small items downtown as she waits for her next bus. This saves her additional miles she would have driven in her car, and it saves her the time of a special trip to the mall. She can read and pray in the bus, which has proven to be another big bonus.

What struck me the most about my conversation with her was her joy. She had learned about God's care for the poor and for the earth, she had prayed about it, and God had led her to do something that reduces pollution and frees up money, which can be given away. Riding the bus isn't something she feels she ought to do. It's something she wants to do because God has led her to do it. It is an act of devotion to God, a way to embrace God's priorities in the world. It has meaning to her because it connects her to God's values and her own values. I believe it is not an accident that she is in her forties as she experiences this combination of discipline, joy and sacrifice for others. It takes most of us a couple of decades of adult life before we can experience that kind of joy when God leads us to do just the right thing.

Many people at midlife have talked with me about the movement in their lives toward experiencing each moment as a gift from God, truly being present to the grace in the small things of life. This involves appreciating the people we are with, paying attention to what we are doing, and noticing the blessings of warmth, beauty and tenderness when they occur in people or in nature. Many people call this attitude "mindfulness."

To the extent that we embrace consumerism, we are forced to speed up the pace of our lives as we need to earn more money to support our lifestyle and spend more time caring for all our possessions. Voluntary simplicity enables us to slow down and experience spaciousness of time and place. Simplicity can help us live more mindfully.

A best-selling writer on simplicity, Cecile Andrews, talks about the fact that our sense of scarcity makes it hard for us to be mindful. We are anxious about time and money; we worry that we won't have enough of either. Our fear of scarcity impacts our whole life and makes us move quickly and frantically. She writes:

> To live mindfully, to appreciate your time, you have to move slowly. There's nothing more difficult for Americans, and we have gotten worse in the last twenty years. Court reporters find that we talk faster. We walk faster, our movies are faster. MTV is the perfect example. Just when you start to focus on an image, the camera moves on.[7]

She advocates saying the words "slow down" almost as a mantra, and she believes that slowing down and practicing mindfulness is a prerequisite for developing an attitude of thankfulness.

God's Gift of a Good Land

For the LORD *your God is bringing you into a good land, a land with flowing streams, with springs and underground waters welling up in valleys and hills, a land of wheat and barley, of vines and fig trees and pomegranates, a land of olive trees and honey, a land where you may eat bread without scarcity, where you will lack nothing, a land whose stones are iron and from whose hills you may mine copper. You shall eat your fill and bless the* LORD *your God for the good land that he has given you. (Deut 8:7-10)*

The Lure of Consumerism

My husband and I have always lived below the standard of living we could afford, and I am deeply grateful for our commitment to that discipline. We have been able to save money for retirement and be generous in giving money away. The pace of our lives has been slower than it might have been if we were driven to earn bigger salaries. That bedrock decision to live frugally, made early in our marriage, has been a wonderful gift that has nurtured simplicity. But . . .

Our lives have grown much more complex, and our lifestyle has escalated as our income has risen. Small decisions have to be made over and over to slow the pace of living, to embrace mindfulness and simplicity. Sometimes it feels as if every day I have to make a deliberate choice to avoid the lure of the consumer culture.

Because we live below our income, recreational shopping is very difficult for me. I see beautiful things, and I want to buy them! Usually I can't use the excuse "I can't afford it," because I could buy much more than I do. The problem is, shopping creates longings and desires that I simply don't want to nurture.

I love buying gifts, because then I can shop with enthusiasm. I enjoy having the excuse to buy things for church ministries. And I do shop when I need specific things for myself. But unless I have a specific agenda, I try to stay out of stores. This is a discipline that I have to choose over and over again. I'll admit it: the materialistic messages of our advertising culture lure me, they call to me. Yet I know that possessions never truly satisfy on any deep or significant level, so (after a few wistful moments) I gladly embrace again my discipline of limited shopping.

A few years ago I quit subscribing to women's magazines. I had always enjoyed reading recipes and looking at the ways people decorate their houses. I began to notice that for me the magazines were creating longings for a nicer house, desires for a bigger kitchen, more expensive furnishings. I don't *want* to want those things, so I decided to eliminate the source of the temptation.

I've also noticed a huge difference in my mood depending on where I walk or bike. Some of the wonderful bike trails in Seattle go through upscale neighborhoods and others through parks. I find that biking or walking among huge and glamorous homes is not nearly as soul-feeding as being in nature, because I so easily find myself lusting after big houses and beautifully manicured gardens, and it takes energy to fight those desires.

In a park I can focus on the ducks on the lake, the clouds in the sky and the wind on my face. There is no way I can possess those things! So I am briefly free from the seductive desires that all too often sweep across my mind. In addition, the creation speaks to me of God's abundance. Nature tells me there is no need for me to accumulate more things, because God my Father already owns all I could need or want. Nature reminds me of God's tender care for me and reinforces the point that I don't need possessions to make me happy. Nature calls me to look for God's hand, listen for God's voice, today—this minute. God is present here and now, and somehow ducks and daffodils help me realize that very real presence.

Recently we moved after living for twelve years in the same house. Despite our commitment to simplicity, and despite being fairly good at getting rid of things, we had accumulated a shocking amount of stuff that we never used. The move was exhausting, partly because we were trying to sort through way too many things and partly because we felt so stupid for having accumulated so much in the first place. Now that we're settled in the new house, surrounded mostly by things that we use and appreciate, there's a sense of serenity that comes to me simply from having things in order. But I know it will not be easy to maintain this uncluttered living. We make choices every day that embrace simplicity or move us toward clutter.

Simplicity and looking for God's hand in creation can reinforce each other in a life-giving ebb and flow. Embracing simplicity can help us slow down enough to hear the voice of creation calling us to draw near to the Creator. At the same time, slowing down enough to appreciate nature can help us desire to get rid of things that clutter our lives and distract us from God. Then we can focus on what is really important to us. At midlife, these complementary forces can be very helpful and encouraging.

Co-Creators with God?

Expressing creativity through art, music, gardening and a host of other avenues is another pathway that can help us connect with God the Creator. And at the same time, allowing ourselves the time and energy to enjoy God's creation can help our own creative juices flow. Just as in the area of simplicity, people at midlife have told me that they experience a vibrant ebb and flow as they enjoy the creation God made and as they engage in creative activities themselves. One feeds on the other.

At the beginning of the chapter we heard from Bill, who talked about the way that the creation speaks to him about God's call to each of us to be creative. As Bill said, we are created in God's image and God is creative. Bill believes that we are all called to be co-creators with God.

Some may object to the term *co-creators*. Clearly we are not equal partners with God in creation. God created and continues to create in a way that is totally different from anything we can do. God creates out of nothing. We take what God has already created, and we create something using already existing forms and objects.

In addition, God sustains the universe in a way that is completely beyond our comprehension and completely different than anything we could do to care for creation. "In him all things hold together," the apostle Paul writes in Colossians 1:17. As much as we might like to exaggerate our own significance in moments of grandiosity, no human being can make that kind of statement about himself or herself.

I experience great joy and a sense of noble challenge when I think of myself as a "co-creator with God." I love the high call to be a partner with God in creating something that reflects God's beauty, love and truth. At the same time, I know I am definitely a junior partner in the endeavor to express God's creativity in human artistry.

I described in chapter two the overwhelming awe I experienced at

39 when I began to write fiction. Truly I felt like a partner with God, making something where nothing had been before. I didn't create the words I used to write stories, but I dreamed up the plots and characters out of nowhere. The exhilarating sense of oneness I experienced with God as I wrote fiction has spilled over into many other areas of life.

For me, writing is a significant creative outlet, whether I'm writing a book, an article or a letter to a friend. In addition, mundane daily activities can call forth my creativity in a way that mirrors God's tender care for creation: fixing a delicious and attractive meal, setting a table with pretty dishes and flowers, arranging a room or choosing flowers for an outdoor pot. I remember reading Edith Schaeffer's classic book *Hidden Art* many years ago. She talks about the artistry that can be expressed in homemaking. Her ideas felt overwhelming to me as a young woman. Now they make sense.

I'm amazed at the number of people I know who enjoy making creative photo albums for their families. I'm also amazed at the number of people who have significant artistic talent for drawing and painting. Every year at Pentecost, we have a "Festival of Gifts" at our church. People bring all kinds of artwork and crafts to show. The variety is amazing. One year a family brought a kayak they had made. The wife does quilting, and a quilt square decorated the front of the kayak, deeply embedded in multiple coats of varnish. One person makes soap. Someone had etched interesting designs on drinking glasses. One person makes little angels as Christmas decorations. One father had made a life-size sculpture of himself and his son, cut out of plywood. People always bring embroidery, quilting, needlepoint, pencil sketches, watercolors, paintings and collages.

I can't say that everyone who brings art or crafts to our Festival of Gifts is at midlife, but many of them are. As the demands of parenting slow down for many during the midlife years, and as we find that work will probably never satisfy our deepest yearnings, we find the time and inclination to discover or resurrect artistic interests. Those artistic interests might be expressed through the visual arts, like so many participants in our Festival of Gifts, but there are many

---

The Animals Teach Us

But ask the animals, and they will teach you;
*   the birds of the air, and they will tell you;*
ask the plants of the earth, and they will teach you;
*   and the fish of the sea will declare to you.*
Who among all these does not know
*   that the hand of the LORD has done this?*
In his hand is the life of every living thing
*   and the breath of every human being. (Job 12:7-10)*

---

other creative outlets: writing poetry, doing woodworking, music, drama, designing gardens, redecorating or remodeling living spaces, sewing, or simply striving to bring beauty and artistry to everyday tasks like cooking or setting a table.

All of these expressions of creativity require slowing down enough to pay attention to something other than the rush and demands of the consumer lifestyle. All of them require standing apart from the pressure and fast pace of so much of life, in order to focus on this immediate expression of beauty. In order to connect with God the Creator by being creative ourselves, it is essential that we embrace simplicity in some form. Simplicity, creative expression through artistic endeavors, and enjoying the creation made by our loving Creator are all intertwined. They build on each other.

In her midlife years, Lorna has discovered a totally new connection with God the Creator. Her story captures many of the issues concerning God and creation that midlife folks have talked to me about.

Lorna's Story

Lorna, 40, is a career counselor.

* * *

I grew up in the suburbs. We moved all the time. I was never encouraged to be in nature. I was actually afraid of nature, wild animals, that kind of thing. Until recently, I had never been camping. I always associated it with being cold, wet and uncomfortable. I think I was afraid of it.

Nature and my physical surroundings were never a part of my awareness. Until only recently, I didn't know the names of the mountain ranges on either side of Seattle. I am now much more aware of the details of nature. The physical world has become a source of comfort to me. I'm much more aware of God's presence in nature. I wonder if this comes from a proximity to death as I grow older.

I came to Christian faith in my teens, and my faith was somehow disembodied. Now I have more of a sense of God's presence in my surroundings. More recently there's been a parallel process of coming into my body. My awareness of God's presence in nature is in response to a need I feel to experience God more tangibly.

I can look at a tree and feel comforted, be reminded to pray. When I look at the tree, there's simplicity. Nature speaks to me of my desire to consume, to comfort myself by buying something. I'm finding I would rather look at the tree than spend the same time shopping.

Every year I see new things in the seasons. Dogwoods. Cherry blossoms. The way they fall on the ground. Kierkegaard says we need to learn from the sparrow, because God cares for each one.

I'm more aware of the moon. When I look at the moon, it feels relational, like God's gift of presence and comfort. I'll always be a talker and will want lots of relationships, but it's like I've found this whole other sense of comfort that helps me connect with myself.

Nature is outside of me, but it connects me to myself. Connecting with nature has given me a developing sense of self, an inner life.

I can be very self-critical and unforgiving to myself. I beat myself up as a Christian that I don't pray enough. Then I look out the window, and the tree ministers to me. Nature communicates grace to me somehow. Nature says, "It's this simple. God is this present."

*   *   *

Questions for Reflection

To think about, write about or talk about with friends.

1. In what ways and in what settings do you experience God's presence in nature? Spend some time thanking God for his handiwork and for the places where you enjoy it most.

2. Is there anything that keeps you from enjoying the creation as God's handiwork? Are you afraid that being too connected to your senses might cause you to sin? Are you concerned that focusing too much on the creation would make you a pantheist? Take these concerns to God in prayer.

3. What choices have you made over the years to try to keep your life simple and uncluttered, with a comfortable pace? In what ways would you like to pursue simplicity and slow down? What are the obstacles?

For Further Reading

From the Bible: Genesis 1—3; Job 38—42; Psalms 19; 104

Cindy Ubben Causey. *Cherish the Gift: A Congregational Guide to Earth Stewardship.* Valley Forge, Penn.: Judson Press, 1996.

Stan L. LeQuire, ed. *The Best Preaching on Earth: Sermons on Caring for Creation.* Valley Forge, Penn.: Judson Press, 1996.

Michael Schut, ed. *Simpler Living, Compassionate Life: A Christian Perspective.* Denver, Colo.: Living the Good News, 1999.

5

Resting in God
Sabbath-Keeping

Twenty years ago my husband and I had the privilege of living in Tel Aviv, Israel, for eighteen months. We expected we would enjoy seeing all the historical sites. We expected it would be interesting to learn about Judaism, to experience a different culture and to watch the amazing interplay of politics and geography in that part of the world.

All of those expectations were met and even surpassed, and we had a wonderfully rich experience in Israel. However, our lives were affected most by something we didn't expect at all: a weekly experience of the Sabbath.

The work week in Israel starts on Sunday morning. On Friday about noon, the work week starts to slow down and people scurry around preparing for the Sabbath. By late afternoon Friday, everyone has finished their weekend shopping. At sunset, the Sabbath begins. Quiet descends on the streets and everything closes until sunset Saturday.

On Sundays, my husband worked all day, and I attended classes. Our church met for worship on Sunday evening. Sunday evening was chosen as the worship time, instead of Saturday, because so many people needed to ride the bus to worship. And throughout

---

Not Just a Day Off

Sabbath is more than the absence of work; it is not just a day off, when we catch up on television or errands. It is the presence of something that arises when we consecrate a period of time to listen to what is most deeply beautiful, nourishing, or true. It is time consecrated with our attention, our mindfulness, honoring those quiet forces of grace or spirit that sustain and heal us.

WAYNE MULLER, *Sabbath: Restoring the Sacred Rhythm of Rest*

Christian history, Sunday worship has been the celebration of the resurrection for most Christians, even if that worship needs to be in the evening.

We lived in an apartment building close to the main road that goes north out of Tel Aviv. All week long, trucks and buses thundered along that road. On the Sabbath, we experienced almost total silence, with only a few cars on the road.

We didn't have a car, so we took the bus everywhere. Because the buses don't run on the Sabbath, our options for recreation were greatly reduced. Besides, where would we go? Grocery stores in our predominantly Jewish neighborhood were closed, along with restaurants, movie theaters and shops. The world simply stopped.

Sometimes a friend with a car would come and pick us up for an outing. Sometimes we rented a car for the weekend to explore some obscure historical site. Sometimes we would make arrangements to get together with friends who lived within walking distance. But most Saturdays we did very little. We slowed down. We read, talked together or walked by the river, which was about a half-mile from our apartment.

All along the river, families would be walking together—children, parents, grandparents. They walked slowly, in no hurry to get somewhere. They were dressed in their finest clothes, and there was a festive air of relaxation and abundance.

Return Home

We returned to the United States excited about the gift we had experienced in being forced to observe a weekly Sabbath. The reduction of options had forced us to slow down dramatically one day each week, and we saw this as a wonderful rhythm that had brought wholeness, balance and emotional health to our lives.

As we began talking about Sabbath observance among our Christian friends, we encountered significant opposition. "That's legalism," people would say. "The New Testament book of Hebrews teaches that our Sabbath rest is fulfilled in Christ. In fact, Jesus healed on the Sabbath and showed us there's no need to observe that part of the Old Testament law."

We tried in vain to describe our experience of the Sabbath as a gift to bring wholeness, rather than some kind of rule to be obeyed. We didn't manage to convince anyone, but we quietly began to establish our own patterns of Sabbath observance.

We decided that Sunday would be our Sabbath and we wouldn't do any work on that day. My husband wouldn't go in to the university to catch up. By then we had a baby and I was going to seminary part-time. I decided I wouldn't do any laundry, grocery shopping or any form of housework on Sundays. I wouldn't study on Sundays. We would attend worship, we decided, and we would enjoy family life for the rest of the day, keeping the pace comfortable and unhurried. If we had company I might do some cooking, but that would be the extent of the work of the day.

On Sundays in our first decade back from Israel, we went for walks, we went to the zoo, we read, we had dinner with friends, we played with our children—now two of them. Because our North American culture doesn't remove options on Sundays as we had experienced in Israel, we removed our own options. We didn't go shopping. We didn't try to do anything productive. And we continued to reap great benefits from this rhythm we had chosen.

As the years passed, an interest in Sabbath observance began to grow among our friends. It appears that many others have discovered the joy of the Sabbath. Books have been published. A few years ago, I was reading an in-flight magazine on a plane trip, and I found an article advocating Sabbath observance. It was written by someone who had been raised Jewish but was no longer observant. Yet she had found that observing the Sabbath had given her space and peace in her busy life.

The Pattern Changes

When I was ordained as a pastor in a congregation a few years ago, we changed our pattern. For me, Sunday mornings are now hard work. I begin my Sabbath mid-afternoon on Sunday, whenever I get home from church. I still take a twenty-four-hour Sabbath. I don't study, read anything related to work, do housework or shop for anything unless absolutely necessary. Mid- to late afternoon on Monday, I begin to organize my desk for the coming week and return phone calls.

During my Sabbath, I seldom turn on my computer. Sometimes I need to check to see if someone has replied to an e-mail. In that case, I'll turn on the computer, look for that one email, and resist the temptation to read the others.

My husband and I spend relaxed time together, often going for a walk or to a movie. I also spend a block of time alone, reading the Sunday paper or a novel. I can feel my body slowing down, so much so that sometimes, if I answer the phone, my speech sounds slurred because I'm thinking so slowly. Often I don't even bother to answer the phone. I let the calls go onto the answering machine to be dealt with later.

In my twenties and thirties, observing the Sabbath felt like a day of joy and grace, a welcome gift from God each week but not actually essential in any way. In my forties, I have come to depend on my Sabbath more deeply. As my strength and energy have begun to slow, I realize how much I need a day of "down time." As my nights are interrupted more often by patches of sleeplessness, I need a day of physical rest. At midlife, observing the Sabbath has become an essential source of rest and renewal.

Why Is Rest Necessary?

The relentless activity that surrounds us lures us into the illusion that we are indispensable. There is something about Western culture in the early twenty-first century that values frantic motion above all else. This high level of productivity and action can subtly reinforce in us false beliefs about ourselves and about God.

At the end of *Perelandra*, the second book in C. S. Lewis's space trilogy, the angels are speaking about God in a majestic ceremony. One angel, addressing the other angels, says that God "has immeasurable use for each thing that is made, that His love and splendour may flow forth like a strong river which has need of a great watercourse. . . . I am infinitely necessary to you."

Another angel responds, saying that God "has no need at all of anything that is made. . . . I am infinitely superfluous, and your love shall be like his, born neither of your need nor of my deserving, but a plain bounty."[1]

This tension, this balance between being necessary and being superfluous, is something we are in danger of losing in our frenetic lifestyles.

God has created us to be his hands and feet on earth, and we are infinitely necessary to God in order to make his love known. As Lewis says, God's love is like a huge river of water that needs a watercourse. We are called to be the watercourse that channels his love to others.

But God is God and we are not. Ultimately, all love comes from him. All love is pure bounty, pure grace. If we spend all our time trying to be faithful and productive, we are in danger of forgetting the depth of our call to be receptive to God's grace. As Dorothy Bass

---

The First Use of "Holy"

One of the most distinguished words in the Bible is the word qadosh, holy; a word which more than any other is representative of the mystery and majesty of the divine. Now what was the first holy object in the history of the world? Was it a mountain? Was it an altar? It is, indeed, a unique occasion at which the distinguished word qadosh is used for the first time: in the book of Genesis at the end of the story of creation. How extremely significant is the fact that it is applied to time: "And God blessed the seventh day and made it holy." There is no reference in the record of creation to any object in space that would be endowed with the quality of holiness.

RABBI ABRAHAM HESCHEL, *The Sabbath*

---

writes, "To act as if the world cannot get along without our work for one day in seven is a startling display of pride that denies the sufficiency of our generous Maker."[2] While God has called us to serve and love in the world as his hands and feet, we are also truly superfluous. Stopping for rest each week can help us hold these two viewpoints in perspective.

Rabbi Abraham Heschel, in his wonderful book *The Sabbath*, writes that we need to learn "to understand that the world has already been created and will survive without the help of man. Six days a week we wrestle with the world, wringing profit from the earth; on the Sabbath we especially care for the seed of eternity planted in the soul."[3]

I live six days each week in the awareness that God has called me to be his faithful servant in the world. I live the seventh day in the awareness that God alone is the giver of every good thing, that he alone runs the universe, and that I am a beloved creature, totally dependent on him as my provider and shepherd.

There is a tradition in Judaism of avoiding intercessory prayer on the Sabbath. It's a day for prayers of praise and thanks, a day to forget the overwhelming needs of the world, a day to focus on the abundance of grace and mercy that God has lavished on us. At midlife more than ever, as the needs of the world are more pressing than they have ever been, most of us are in desperate need of that kind of perspective.

My Favorite Sabbath Story

Several years ago I heard someone tell a fascinating story that illustrates the benefits of keeping the Sabbath. The setting is the Oregon Trail days around 1850. A large wagon train of over 150 people set off from St. Louis. The leader was devoted to keeping the Sabbath, and he had talked over his plan with the whole group before they left. Every week on Sunday, the wagon train would stay where they were. They would give their animals and themselves a chance to rest.

A couple of weeks passed. Each Sunday, the people in the wagon train stayed in their camp in the middle of nowhere, with nothing much to do, watching the other wagon trains pass them by. At this rate, some of them felt sure, they would never get to Oregon.

A splinter group decided to break off from the main group and travel seven days a week. They said, "Why should we let those other wagon trains pass us by? We'll get there faster if we travel seven days a week." On the next Sunday, that group sped ahead while the main group rested. But after a few weeks, the main group—the Sabbath-keeping group—passed the splinter group, and the main group arrived in Oregon City without seeing the splinter group again.

The women and children stayed in Oregon City while the men went back to try to help the splinter group. They found them stuck in the Blue Mountains in eastern Oregon, their animals exhausted and the people lagging. With the help of the extra men, they were able to regain some energy and straggle into Oregon City.

I can't document this story. But I like it because it illustrates my experience with Sabbath-keeping. It also reminds me of my college days. In the Christian fellowship group on my campus, we were told that we should have a quiet time every day, whether or not we felt pressured to study. We would find, we were told, that in the long run we actually got more done. That was certainly true for me.

As a busy student, I found that a half-hour each day reading the Bible and praying quieted my mind. It helped me see more clearly what I should do and not do. I experienced God's companionship and power more vividly on the days when I had spent time quietly with God. I didn't spin my wheels doing needless tasks. I was focused, directed, energetic and productive. I came to see clearly that sometimes when I was the most pressured and busy, that was the time to stop and do nothing for a while, to rest in God's presence and seek his leading. The Sabbath functions the same way in our weekly rhythm of life.

A purist might argue that we are called to observe the Sabbath because we should obey God, and God says we are to rest on the Sabbath. While this is true, I am grateful that we can also enumerate distinct benefits from Sabbath observance. In his conflicts with the religious leaders about what was appropriate on the Sabbath, Jesus said, "The Sabbath was made for humankind, not humankind for the Sabbath" (Mk 2:27). The Sabbath wasn't made so we can have a set of rules to obey. It was created as a gift for us so that we can enjoy the balance between work and rest for which God created us. When I miss my Sabbath because of some unexpected and unavoidable event, I can see clearly that I have less energy and direction than usual all week.

Why Adopt a Sabbath at Midlife?

As I have gotten older, I feel more like one of those tired horses on the Oregon Trail. Day after day there is so much to be done. The responsibilities have piled up as the years have piled up. And, at the same time, I simply have fewer recuperative powers than I had when I was younger.

I watch my two sons, both in their early twenties. They push themselves mercilessly, and then they sleep until noon or sometimes even until late afternoon. They drive to Southern California nonstop from Seattle. They catch catnaps in the car and then sleep twelve or fourteen hours after they arrive. Then they're fine!

When I get exhausted, I simply don't recover very fast any more. I can't sleep in the car very easily. I can't sleep until noon or late afternoon. I can't catch up on rest in one huge sleep orgy. I need patterns of rest that will sustain me for the long haul. The Sabbath is part of the rhythm that I need for health and energy. In my midlife years, I need it more than ever.

The Sabbath provides us with a structure in which to learn to slow down. Seminary professor Bonnie Thurston writes, "When we slow down, when we become attentive to the present, when we are rooted in today, in the here-and-now, we permit God to 'break through' into our awareness." She continues, "If we don't find God in this present moment, we are unlikely to encounter the Divine at all. St. Paul deeply understood this truth and wrote to the Corinthians, 'See, now is the acceptable time; see, now is the day of salvation!' (2 Cor 6:2)."[4]

At midlife, as commitments and responsibilities have become more complex, and as life seems to spin faster and faster, we need the help of a structure to enable us to make space for God. The Sabbath gives us time each week for the kind of slowing down that is necessary to encounter God. The Sabbath trains our minds and souls in the art of creating space for God. The turn inward that is so common at midlife provides the perfect soil in which to grow the discipline of

Sabbath-keeping. And Sabbath observance will spill over into daily life a greater attentiveness to God in each moment of the day.

Many of the writers on the Sabbath, while affirming the need for a weekly commitment to a Sabbath, also advocate taking little Sabbaths each day. It may be a daily quiet time, as mentioned above, consisting of Bible study and prayer. Or there may simply be moments of quiet, of rest and slowing down, which happen spontaneously during the day. One friend finds that when she parks her car at a shopping mall to do an errand, she often can spare five to seven minutes before jumping out to shop. She simply reclines the seat a bit and sits there in the sun (radio turned off) to think or pray or just *be*.

As I have continued to grow in my appreciation for my husband's and my Sabbath discipline, and as I have learned to slow down even more on the Sabbath, I have noticed the way the moments of quiet have spilled over into my daily life. As I am waiting in line at the bank, I can feel myself begin to fidget. Then I remind myself that here is a precious moment when I can quiet my heart before God and receive grace and love. Here is a small piece of time where I can practice being superfluous, being receptive to the reality of God's initiating love irrespective of my achievements. I watch other people standing in line talking on their cell phones, and I feel sorrow that nothing in our culture encourages the kind of quiet that enables us to receive God's love.

At midlife, many people become more aware of time. We realize afresh that our time on earth is limited, and therefore our time is precious in a way we hadn't really believed before. One day we will live in heaven, which is outside time. *What is life like outside time?* we wonder. If we become more connected to nature, we thus experience more deeply the rhythms of the seasons, of planting and harvesting, of death and rebirth.

Observing a weekly Sabbath rhythm can help us make sense of time in a new way. We, like all animals and plants, are now participating in a rhythm that builds on the way we were created. Because each week we experience one day of being receptive to God's love rather than totally absorbed with what we have to do, we are preparing for heaven. Abraham Heschel goes so far as to say that the Sabbath is a little taste of eternal life, and unless we can enjoy it on earth, we certainly won't find ourselves enjoying it once we are in heaven![5]

The Sabbath
Six days shall work be done, but the seventh day is a sabbath of solemn rest, holy to the LORD. (Ex 31:15)
For thus said the Lord GOD, the Holy One of Israel:
In returning and rest you shall be saved;
*   in quietness and in trust shall be your strength. (Is 30:15)*
Thus says the LORD:
Stand at the crossroads, and look,
*   and ask for the ancient paths,*
where the good way lies; and walk in it,
*   and find rest for your souls.*
But they said, "We will not walk in it." (Jer 6:16)

Sometimes I think our culture's frantic activity is rooted in a fear of slowing down, a fear of exposing that we aren't as competent as we appear, a fear that we might encounter something negative in ourselves or we might hear from God in a threatening way. As we navigate the midlife years, learning to be more honest about ourselves, we realize that even people of faith are prey to those fears. We become more aware that we are possessive, worried, achievement-oriented people who want to earn respect and adulation just like anyone else.

The Sabbath is a day to let go of all that. Imagine having a day each week when you have the freedom to ignore the seductive desires that sweep across your mind, the liberty not to work at anything at all, and permission not to worry. *Should we remodel our kitchen?* As the thought gathers force in my mind, a series of ensuing thoughts pursue that initial idea: *Do we have enough money? Is it materialistic to want a nicer kitchen? How nice should it be? What exactly should we do or not do?* On any normal day of the week, I will usually let those kinds of thoughts gather in my mind, and I can easily become preoccupied with the question I'm tussling with. As I drive to work, I stew about the question. I wake up at night, worried about it. I might look at our saving account to see about the money. I might call a friend who's a contractor to talk about costs.

But on the Sabbath, as those kind of thoughts begin to flow, I tell myself, "You can think about this another day. Not today." It's not easy to let go of our desires, but it does get easier with practice. The discipline of setting them aside one day each week will bear very good fruit. We really can become more attentive to the things that truly matter to us.

It takes planning and discipline to achieve a weekly Sabbath with that kind of freedom, but it can be done. It doesn't mean that every moment of a Sabbath day will be filled with perfect freedom from worry and fleeting seductive desires, with perfect awareness of God's grace and love. But there will be very, very good moments.

Candles and Other Ways to Welcome the Sabbath

In the Jewish tradition, the Sabbath is viewed as a queen to be welcomed with candles, a lovely meal, clean and festive clothes and special prayers. For Christians as well, symbols can be very helpful in setting apart this special time.

Candles are particularly well suited to marking the Sabbath. Kids love candles and enjoy festivities that involve candles. The symbolism of light connects us to the reality of God's light in our lives. On the Sabbath as we celebrate the good gifts of God, what better symbol of God's abundance can there be than to watch light spread from one candle to the next in a dim room?

At the ecumenical Taizé community in France, the Sabbath is welcomed each week with candlelight spreading in a dark sanctuary. Some families adopt the Jewish tradition of having the mother light three candles. Others use one candle for each family member, as a symbol of God's presence with each one. Single people have also spoken to me about the significance of candles as they begin the Sabbath on their own. The presence of God and his loving companionship seem more real when they light a Sabbath candle.

Any prayer that affirms God's light can be used along with the candle-lighting. Psalms 29, 92 and 93 are traditionally associated with the Sabbath, but any psalm can be used to begin or end Sabbath time. Special prayers welcoming the Sabbath can be used.

In the Jewish tradition, prayers of blessing for the children may be recited at the beginning of the Sabbath. Children are usually very open to participating in prayers that ask God to bless them! A special meal and special clothes can also help children grasp the festiveness of the day and help adults lay aside the worries and preoccupations of the week.

The Jewish tradition also has patterns for ending the Sabbath: lighting a multiwicked candle, smelling a box full of spices and drinking a glass of wine. There's a sense of sadness as the Sabbath ends, and a desire for God's quickening of our abilities and energy as we enter another work week.

Sabbath Time

Some Christian Sabbath observers keep the Jewish Sabbath, from sundown Friday evening through sundown Saturday evening. Some adapt it to include Sunday worship, by beginning their Sabbath on Saturday evening and ending it on Sunday evening. There is a significant advantage to beginning the Sabbath at sundown. You can mark the beginning of the Sabbath with candles in the darkness, and you can welcome the Sabbath with a special meal.

Others pick a Sabbath day that fits their work schedule. Eugene Peterson, a pastor for many years, has written in several of his books about his Sabbath pattern as a pastor. He and his wife observed Mondays as their Sabbath. Typically they would go on a long walk in the country, keeping silence on the way out and then sharing talk on the way back. As mentioned earlier, my Sabbath used to be all day Sunday and now it begins Sunday afternoon and ends Monday afternoon.

The important factor is length of time. It really does take a whole twenty-four-hour period to follow the Sabbath patterns of relinquishment and rest.

Retreat director Tilden Edwards notes that Sabbath observance will always have a negative and a positive dimension.[6] First we will decide how we are going to set our Sabbath time apart from other time. What options will we remove in order to set aside our role as a productive, hard-working person? What aspects of our everyday life will we choose to eliminate on Sabbath days? After we decide what to say no to, then we say yes. We have to decide what to include in the time, in order to fill the space with God's presence and all the joys of rest, joy, connectedness and intimacy that come with an authentic experience of God.

What to Drop on the Sabbath

The Old Testament Sabbath laws involve curtailing work. What constitutes work for you? Certainly you will want to consider eliminating whatever you do to earn money during your work week.

Because my first decade of Sabbath observance occurred when I was not employed, I developed an understanding of work that involves far more than our efforts to earn money. For me, work includes tidying up, laundry, cleaning house, shopping for groceries, taking my car in for an oil change and balancing the checkbook.

Work also includes thinking about the next class I'm going to teach, planning next year's household budget in my head and musing about the pros and cons of remodeling our kitchen.

For the past decade, as I have had a home office and done a lot of writing and editing at home, I have had an additional Sabbath challenge. Am I going to walk into my home office on my Sabbath? Am I going to begin to read miscellaneous unopened mail on my desk and thus get sucked into filing things and making notes of things to do? Am I going to turn on the computer just to write a note to a friend but then get drawn into reading e-mail related to work?

Much of what my husband and I experienced when we were so profoundly affected by the Sabbath atmosphere in Israel was the removal of options. Stores were closed; public transportation wasn't running. We have tried to bring that same spirit to our Sabbaths. It's just not an option for me to sit at my desk and do anything productive, whether it relates to a paid job or our household finances. This removal of options is more significant than ever before during the midlife years, when a multitude of options and responsibilities swirl around us every day and in every setting.

We were also impacted by the way we saw people are scurrying around on Friday afternoons getting groceries and flowers, preparing food in advance for the Sabbath. When the Sabbath starts, there is a huge moment of relaxation, of slowing down. Now the rest begins. Now the relaxation begins.

On Fridays now, I begin noticing what needs to be done to prepare for the Sabbath. Are we getting low on milk or fruit? I don't want to run out of something essential on Sunday, so I make plans to shop for whatever we need in advance of Sunday. I usually spend some time tidying up on Saturday, so I won't be tempted to do so on Sunday. I often check my e-mail late on Saturday afternoon, because I know I won't look at it again until late Monday afternoon, and I don't want something urgent to get ignored. Sometimes I cook a large meal on

Friday or Saturday, so there will be leftovers for Sunday and I won't have to cook.

Wayne Muller, author of *Sabbath: Restoring the Sacred Rhythm of Rest*, suggests a way to begin observing the Sabbath. Choose one heavily used appliance, he recommends, and let it rest on the Sabbath. It might be the telephone, television, washer and dryer or computer.[7] You might begin with one and see how it feels after a few months.

The use of media is a significant Sabbath question. Some people feel that the single most oppressive aspect of our culture is our aggressive, sex-permeated media. A Sabbath from media might be another place to start, taking one day each week to turn off the TV and radio, set aside the newspaper and ignore any magazines sitting around the house. At the same time, watching a movie or video that is relaxing and fun can be a good Sabbath activity, and many people enjoy the opportunity to read the Sunday paper in a leisurely manner.

Shopping on the Sabbath raises another interesting question. Buying groceries certainly qualifies as work in my mind, but a leisurely shopping expedition might be restful and fun. I wish that stores weren't open on Sundays so everyone could have time to rest with their families, so I try not to shop on Sundays at all. In addition, the acquisitiveness and materialism that shopping elicits in me require some degree of effort to combat. I simply don't want to work that hard on my Sabbath, so I have decided not to shop at all, if possible, on my Sabbath.

I once read an article about a man who decided not to talk on Sundays. He felt that his life was so full of words that they had lost their value. As the weeks and months went by, he realized how much he enjoyed being free to explore his thoughts without having to say anything about them, so he kept this habit for many years. His family adjusted to his silence pretty easily.

If part of the purpose of the Sabbath is to increase intimacy and connection with people we love, then stopping all conversation might be counterproductive for most of us. It's still worth considering what the man did. He evaluated his life and found an aspect of it that was in danger of becoming meaningless because of overuse. At midlife, when the search for meaning is becoming more intense and when so many aspects of our lives are in danger of becoming trivial because of overuse, we can find balance and a renewed sense of values by consciously choosing to eliminate on the Sabbath something that we do too often.

What kind of balance do you need in your life? What aspect of your life is in danger of meaninglessness because of overuse? What are the characteristics of your six days of work? If you work alone, then maybe what you need on the Sabbath is time with people. If your life is full of people, then maybe on the Sabbath you need a block of time alone. If your life is very sedentary, then maybe your Sabbath rest needs to include a lot of physical activity. If you are physically active at work, or if you are devoted to regular physical fitness, your Sabbath may need to include a lot of physical rest. Deciding what boundaries to put around your Sabbath activities involves looking carefully at your life.

What to Do on the Sabbath

As Tilden Edwards points out, first we have to decide what we're not going to do on the Sabbath, and then we decide what we *will* do. An attitude of experimentation is very valuable here. Maybe you decide to try long hikes on the Sabbath, and then you find you're too tired when Monday comes. Try something else! There are a variety of possibilities: reading alone or out loud, games with family or friends, outings to the zoo or museums, day trips to the country, gourmet cooking, gardening and a hundred other things.

Gardening provides a great example of the fact that one person's rest and recreation is another person's work. For me, gardening is part of the work of caring for our house. I enjoy aspects of gardening, just as I might enjoy redecorating a room, but most gardening feels like work to me. I almost never garden on my Sabbath.

But gardening is the most popular recreational activity in the United States. For many people, uninterrupted hours in the garden

---

Revealing God's Love

The Sabbath expresses the heart of the Good News, that God in Christ reveals an infinite love for us that does not depend on our works. It depends simply on our willingness for it, on our desire to turn to that Great Love with our deepest love, through all our little loves. Thus observance of the Sabbath has an evangelical dimension. What better way to reveal God's love beyond our works than to stop our usual works and discover that Love is not withdrawn, but strongly visible for us? Not only is this a witness for ourselves, but also for others as they see us intentionally celebrating an identity and love that is not dependent on our worthy productions. In our simple Sabbath rest, doing nothing but appreciating the giftedness of life in God, we can reveal the Gospel to our neighbors in a demonstrable, non-aggressive, yet very challenging way.

TILDEN EDWARDS, *Sabbath Time*

---

are delightful, a kind of rest that involves physical exercise, exposure to beauty, and use of creativity. Gardening might be a great thing for some people to do on their Sabbath.

The challenge with any Sabbath activity is to keep it from becoming work. Keep it leisurely. Go at a pace that's slow enough to allow yourself to truly enjoy what you're going. Don't multitask; focus on only one thing at a time.

The Sabbath, Tilden Edwards writes, "is a time for 'useless' poetry and other arts; a time to appreciate a tree, your neighbor, yourself without doing something to them; a time to praise God as an end it itself. It is a time for superfluous—overflowing the merely necessary—movements, meetings and worlds."[8] What activity do you consider to be superfluous, totally unnecessary and unproductive? Maybe that's what you need to do on your Sabbath.

The Sabbath and Kids

As I've talked with people about Sabbath-keeping, a good number of parents have told me that keeping a Sabbath would be impossible for them because they have children—active, noisy, busy, energetic kids who demand a lot of attention each and every day. Often, they tell me, their kids have sports activities on both Saturday and Sunday. I know that children's energy and sports commitments make life complicated, but they certainly don't rule out the possibility of Sabbath observance.

Parents of very young children definitely have challenges on the Sabbath, because the work of caring for little ones never stops. I benefited a great deal when my children were young from a Sabbath discipline of avoiding housework and shopping on the Sabbath and really trying to enjoy time with the kids without pressure to get anything else done.

All the sporting events on Sundays present another challenge. I've driven my kids to countless sporting events, and I remember clearly the way it usually happened. We were in a hurry, rushing out the door at the last minute. I usually had an errand to run on the way there or on the way home. I would often take something productive to do while I watched the practices or games.

How could it be different on the Sabbath? First, avoid multitasking. Don't run any errands on the way to and from the game. Take along some well-loved poetry or a fun novel to read at the game; don't take anything productive to do. If the weather is nice, leave home half an hour early and lie in the grass with your child watching the clouds. Or take along a picnic to share with your child before or after the game. Slow down. Make it fun and relaxing. Make it the only event of the day. Do it together as a family.

Teenagers are another question. After years of Sabbath observance as a family, they will likely no longer want to be included. Each parent has to make their own decision about how much to insist on participation with the family. As our children grew more independent, my husband and I explored new ways of observing the Sabbath, spending more time as a couple and also spending time alone. Nothing stays the same. What works one year might not work the next.

Our culture wants to make us into leisure machines. When we're not working, our culture tells us, we're supposed to be consuming leisure activities at the same furious pace that the working world requires. The Sabbath is a way to step outside all of that. Sure, we might engage in leisure activities on the Sabbath, but we need to grow in doing them with a quiet, joyous, noncompetitive spirit.

One Family's Story

Sam and Lois are both 42. Sam is a pastor and Lois is an artist. Two and a half years ago they started observing a Sabbath, along with their children, who are 9, 11 and 14.

*   *   *

LOIS: We had been interested in the possibility of observing the Sabbath for several years. We read books and debated how to do it. Could we have a Sabbath with Sam as a pastor? I could feel resistance in myself also. How could I spend a day without being productive? How could we ask the kids not to do homework for a day? Finally we decided, let's just start with what we've got. We can make it a day to stop in some way and to pray together at the beginning and end. We can set some basic guidelines and see how it grows.

SAM: Beginning a Sabbath was a lot more casual than you would think. We are always looking for things we can do together as a family that connect faith with our kids. This changes as the kids get older, and it seemed the time was right to try something new.

LOIS: We sat down with the kids and talked to them about the possibility of keeping the Sabbath. We framed it in a really positive way—look at this gift God has given us. We've never really grabbed onto it before, but we could now. We told them that the Sabbath is a wonderful thing. It's not that we're going to tell you what not to do, we're going to do really fun things. It will involve a fun meal at home or out, as a family or with friends. We decided not to make the meal a bunch of work for me, so the meals are simple if we eat at home. We don't want to eat out all the time.

SAM: The kids were okay with the idea. We've prayed together as a family enough, so they thought the idea of a brief prayer time at the beginning would be okay. We got the most resistance from our oldest child. "I've got a life," he said, "and I need to do homework on Sundays." We responded, "What if you thought about it this way: here's a period of time when you wouldn't have to study. You could ride your bike, relax, shoot baskets, play with friends without the pressure of studying hanging over you." It was like a light bulb going on. We could see the moment when he understood this might be a gift.

LOIS: We've developed the evening part. We begin our Sabbath on Saturday evening.

SAM: I call the Saturday evening part our family "Sabbath time."

LOIS: We keep one candle that's just for the Sabbath. We gather before dinner. We light that candle, and Sam leads us in a breathing prayer. We imagine we are breathing in the peace of Christ and breathing out the stresses of our life. If we miss that part, the kids remind us to do it. Someone grabs a Bible and we read a passage from the Psalms or maybe Isaiah. It's not very long. Then we talk about the verse for a few minutes. Someone prays for the Sabbath.

SAM: Our family Sabbath time points us to the idea that now we're starting a different kind of time. It feels freeing to give yourself to a different time. We try to keep the start of the Sabbath together. If one kid is going to a friend's house for the evening or to a ball game, we might move up our family Sabbath time to five p.m. instead of six p.m. so we can all be together.

LOIS: Preparation is important. An hour or two before the Sabbath time we negotiate with the kids. Is there homework you need to get done before the Sabbath starts? I try to have all the laundry done, and Sam tries to have his sermon finished.

SAM: We haven't structured the whole twenty-four-hour Sabbath a lot. We haven't told the kids they have to do certain activities or they always have to be with us as a family. The only thing we've insisted on is no homework, because we felt that for kids, studying is their work.

LOIS: When we first talked about keeping a Sabbath, the kids decided themselves that they wouldn't do homework, and they really own that now. We try to do stuff as a family on Sunday afternoon. If someone's doing a sport, we all try to go. On the other days of the week, if someone stays home, it's to do homework. On Sundays they are free not to have to do that.

SAM: People always ask me how I can preach on Sundays and still call it my Sabbath. I really enjoy preaching, and I feel privilege and pleasure in it. I view the preparation for preaching as the work, and I try to have that done by Saturday afternoon. I love beginning the Sabbath on Saturday evening with my family. On Sundays, I really enter into the worship services. Each Sunday I feel like I have been with Christ in worship, which is a big part of the Sabbath. I try to not schedule meetings on Sundays, and sometimes I don't attend meetings that others have scheduled. I protect Sunday afternoons for my family.

LOIS: At the end of the Sabbath, we light the Sabbath candle again. We're not as consistent here, but we try. We share about the favorite moment we each experienced during the last twenty-four hours, and then we have a quick prayer of thankfulness. During Sunday afternoon, I can feel the week stacking up ahead of me, but I just don't touch it until after Sunday dinner when our Sabbath is over.

SAM: Observing the Sabbath has had many different impacts on us. I love the family Sabbath times. Some of the best ones have been when we've had guests for dinner. Some guests have been Christian, some non-Christian, and we've kept our Sabbath time very casual with guests. I can see the impact on them. There's something about beginning the Sabbath together that's so countercultural. I like that. We conform to our culture in so many areas, and it's nice to have something for a change where we can say that the rest of life can work around this.

LOIS: Recently our older son, our most focused and intense child, described to us the gift that the Sabbath is for him. He said, "It's a day where I can't stress about my homework." He loves the Sabbath. It gives him the day off. He can't allow himself to take time off on his own. He loves the joy of rest that he can't choose on his own. We've never forced the kids to be obedient to the Sabbath, but he takes it very seriously.

SAM: The ability to give myself to the Sabbath has affected the quiet times I try to have every morning. By observing the Sabbath, I have learned to say to myself, "This is a different kind of time." Now each morning as I turn to Scripture reading, prayer and journaling, I say that, and it enables me to resist running into my office to check my e-mail. It enables me to be more present to God.

LOIS: For me, the Sabbath has reframed Sunday in a very nice way. Because I was raised outside the church, I have always resisted the amount of time that Sunday church services take. For the first time in my life, my whole being enjoys going to worship because it's placed well within the space I've been given for the Sabbath. When we light the Sabbath candle on Saturday night, I can feel the stress deflate, and that makes Sunday a day outside of time. On the other six days, life feels like a continuum where you're either getting ahead or falling behind. Now, on Sundays there's no need to accomplish anything. I'm a person who has a hard time taking time just for myself, but in this case, the time is just there. And it's so wonderful to have a spiritual practice we all do together.

SAM: It's no accident that we were at midlife when we began observing the Sabbath. We had lived long enough to experience that crazy flip-flop that humans do, bouncing back and forth between living by grace and living by discipline. By the time midlife arrived, I had achieved some kind of integration of the two. I could say to my family, "We're going to keep the Sabbath in a disciplined way with some degree of structure, but we understand that it's our desire for God that is driving our Sabbath practice, not legalism or rules."

LOIS: At midlife, we could finally catch our breath as parents. We looked back over the years of fun and chaos with little people in our home, and we looked ahead to the priorities and values we wanted our kids to take away as adults from our family times together. We felt called to a new sense of being intentional in what we communicate to them about God, not just in words, but also in what we do. The Sabbath has been a wonderful framework and structure for that expression.

* * *

Questions for Reflection
To think about, write about or talk about with friends.

1. In what ways do you need more rest? What kind of rest do you need? Do you have emotions of guilt or fear associated with the need for rest? What are the roots of those emotions? Take these concerns to God in prayer.

2. What early lessons did you learn about the Sabbath? In what ways do those lessons impact your life now?

3. If you could try one thing to begin to observe a Sabbath, or to amplify your current Sabbath observance, what would it be? What are the obstacles to taking that step? What might be the blessings of taking that step?

For Further Reading
Tilden Edwards. *Sabbath Time*. Nashville: Upper Room, 1992.

Abraham Joshua Heschel. *The Sabbath.* New York: Farrar, Straus & Giroux, 1951.

Wayne Muller. *Sabbath: Restoring the Sacred Rhythm of Rest.* New York: Bantam, 1999.

Don Postema. *Catch Your Breath: God's Invitation to Sabbath Rest.* Grand Rapids, Mich.: CRC Publications, 1997.

Bonnie Thurston. *To Everything a Season: A Spirituality of Time.* New York: Crossroad, 1999.

6

Embracing Discipline
Benedictine Spirituality

I've decided to come with you to the monastery again this year. Last year I was able to pray there in a way I've never experienced before."

For several years I have taken a group of women from our congregation to a Benedictine monastery for women in Idaho for a weekend. When I walk into the monastery, I have a strong sense that people have prayed in this place for many, many years, and that I will be able to pray there too. I was glad when one of the young women at church confirmed my experience.

Last year when we toured the monastery during our visit, one of the sisters said that Benedictine life is all about sacred places and sacred times, and indeed it is the serenity of place and the rhythm of time that are most noticeable to a visitor. I have stayed in monasteries housed in large building with "chapels" that look like small cathedrals, and I have also stayed in a monastery in a large house with a chapel in the basement. What they have in common is a sense of the space being consecrated to prayer and to prayerful work.

What's also striking about monasteries is the schedule of prayer services. Some have the traditional seven services each day, some five, some two or three, but in every case the prayer services—also called the divine office or liturgy of the hours—set a rhythm for daily life.

In addition, immediately visible is the spirit of hospitality. Guests are to be welcomed as if they were Christ himself. Most monasteries devote space to guest quarters and expect that hosting guests will be a significant ministry for them.

The priorities of prayer and hospitality are rooted in the *Rule of St. Benedict*, a foundation that lies behind most monastic life today. Benedict's balanced view of life calls monks and sisters to a rhythm and order that are visible when visiting a monastery. It may seem that these monastic patterns have nothing to do with the ordinary daily life that most of us experience at our jobs or in our families. Yet many people at midlife have talked with me about the ways they have been impacted by visits to monasteries. They have enjoyed the quiet and reflection while they are there, and they have also carried something significant back home with them.

The popularity of Kathleen Norris's books is one indication of a growing awareness that we have something important to learn from the monastic tradition. Norris writes in several of her books about her experiences staying at Benedictine monasteries. What she has learned in those visits has spilled over into her daily life. In Brian's story, we will see the way the visit to a monastery called him to reexamine several aspects of his daily life.

Brian's Story

Brian, 46, is an attorney. He has spent time at two different monasteries, ranging from a few days to a week each time. Here's how he describes his first visit.

*   *   *

My first monastery experience came six or seven years ago, right before a sabbatical I was taking from my law firm. I experienced a kind of tinderbox tension leading up to the sabbatical, trying to get everything done, trying not to leave too many unfinished projects for others to complete. As I drove home from work that last day, I was still dictating letters and leaving voice mails via my car phone.

As I drove to the monastery the next day, I was revved on coffee, full of energy, playing loud music on my car stereo. As I followed the road up the hill to the monastery through the cool woods, I could feel myself unwind. There's an open place at the top, where the breeze was blowing. I stopped my car and sat, feeling the quiet. Under the quiet, I could feel waves and waves of fatigue. Under the fatigue, I could feel waves and waves of emptiness.

In my week at the monastery, God showed his love to me.

In Benedict's *Rule*, there is no vow of silence, but there is a presumption against speaking. Speech is reserved for necessary things only, and there is a healthy understanding of the dangers of the tongue.

During my week at the monastery, I had a few mealtime conversations, but by and large I didn't talk to anyone for a week. In the space where words would have been, there was room for God.

The silence didn't scare me like it might have at a younger age. As you get older, you just get worn out from the noise. Life exhausts you. The pace exhausts you. So you are drawn to a place where you perceive it might be different, where it might be quiet.

It doesn't mean it was necessarily easy. God was working with me that week. There were tears even as I was journaling.

I noted the role work plays in a monastery. To an outsider, it's clear that work is a minor part of the picture. It's a way to fill time between prayer services, a way for the monks to support themselves, a way to fill in the edges between what's important.

At the monastery I visited, the monks attend a series of seven prayer services every day, beginning at 5:30 a.m. and ending at 7:00 p.m. These prayer services created an incredible sense of rhythm for me. I knew I would be anchored in prayer continually. The services integrated God into the whole day. And it seemed that for the monks, their lives are knit together into one whole, not fragmented. They work in order to be able to pray. My life at home—work, family, PTA, church—it has God over top of it all, but it still seems fragmented. I pray in order to be able to work.

I was struck by the monks' approach to time. It is not adversarial. While I was at the monastery, God was showing me that I always fight time, trying to manage it, buy it, control it. I have too much time or too little time. I'm always struggling with it. The monks always seem to have enough time, just the right amount of time. No one rushes. They live in a rhythm that seems unforced.

I enjoyed the sense of rhythm. The monks go back and forth between work and prayer and rest. Time is seen as rhythmical rather than linear. It was clear to me that in our everyday lives we try to control time with our schedules.

At one meal I had an interesting conversation with a monk who works in the book bindery at the monastery. I asked him, "What if you were trying to meet a FedEx deadline and the bells rang for the prayer service? What would you do? Would you keep on working to meet the deadline? Would you choose to miss the deadline and go to the prayer service? How would you decide?"

The monk looked at me as if I were out of my mind. They really don't understand the drive to squeeze things in because they don't live that way.

*   *   *

Benedict

Benedict of Nursia, who lived from about 480 to 547, was by no means the first monk interested in monastic communal living. As early as the second century after Christ, individual Christians left the comforts and stresses of society to pursue a life of solitary prayer in the wilderness. When more Christians joined them, all the issues of community living presented themselves. Benedict's *Rule* was based on earlier writings that gave guidelines for communal Christian living.

Benedict belongs to all Christians, of course, since he lived a thousand years before the church divided into Catholics and Protestants. The *Rule of St. Benedict* has depth, balance and a practical orientation that changed the face of spirituality in the Western half of the Christian world.

The *Rule*, a short book composed of a prologue and seventy-three brief chapters, addresses everyday topics: work, recreation, food, silence, rest, study, prayer, and the need to listen. There are some sections that prescribe discipline and daily routines in a way that is foreign to us, but much of the *Rule* is still applicable today for monastic living and presents significant insights even for those of us who are not called to a monastery.

Benedict lays out three monastic vows: stability, conversion of life, and obedience. All of these have practical application in everyday life for any Christian. Benedict believed that we have enough—that God has given us all we need for our daily lives. Knowing that helps us slow down our striving and enables us to look for God in the everyday aspects of living. Benedict calls us to the disciplines of prayer, self-examination and confession, all of them exercised in community.

Perhaps the current interest in Benedictine community living comes in part because of the parallels between Benedict's time and ours. In his early adulthood in Italy, Benedict became so disillusioned and disgusted with the affluence and decadence of his society that he withdrew to an isolated cave to live a solitary life of prayer. Other people soon joined him for much the same reasons, and a monastic community began to grow. The *Rule* was written to guide the community as its life developed.

Benedict lived in a time of affluence and sophistication in the Roman Empire. Wealth was used unscrupulously for personal political gain, the gap between the rich and the poor was widening and the church was infected with controversy and political concerns. Child slavery, prostitution, oppression and injustice permeated society. Barbarian tribes from the north were migrating into the settled, agrarian lands of northern Italy, producing a multicultural society characterized by change and instability.

Our times are not much different. The genius of Benedict's *Rule* comes from its simplicity and its call back to the basics of Scripture, prayer, solitude, community and service, which transcend political turmoil and cultural upheaval. The *Rule* offers guidelines for ordinary people living ordinary lives. At midlife, the simplicity of Benedict's priorities can enable us to center our lives in Christ in the midst of the many responsibilities, priorities and commitments that are so common in the midlife years.

Monastic Living for Ordinary Life

Paul Wilkes, a Catholic writer and teacher, wrote a very helpful book called *Beyond the Walls: Monastic Wisdom for Everyday Life*. He describes his several attempts to become a Trappist monk. The Trappists are a monastic order based on the principles of Benedict's *Rule*. Wilkes spent extended periods of time living at a Trappist monastery, hoping to receive a call from God to monastic life.

Instead he received a call to marriage and parenthood. He continues to spend time regularly at a Trappist monastery located several hours from his home, and the basic disciplines of monastic living have flowed into his everyday life, giving structure, joy and stability to his family life and his work.

On one recent visit to the monastery, he was daydreaming during a prayer service. His eyes wandered up to a round window high in the cupola of the chapel. Bright white clouds danced across a deep blue sky, and he realized how well he could see the clouds and how bright were the colors because his view was restricted to a little piece of sky. He writes, "Such it is with the monastic life; so restricted, a small, pure peephole on the universe—but what a view! Profound, rich, more than enough for human eyes to behold. We need to restrict the view in order to better see the movement of God; by seeing everything, we see nothing at all." He saw clearly that his own life, with all its wanderings until he settled down to family life in his late forties, was "living proof of that."[1]

On another visit, he was struggling with the tepid nature of his experience of God. He felt his prayers were almost always one-sided, too many frantic words directed to God with very few answers in return. He deeply wanted his faith to flow over into his life more and more, but he continued to experience irritation, lack of patience, and anger. He wanted a deeper experience of God that would transform him.

He talked with Paul, a wheelchair-bound monk, about his concerns.

"Don't go at it so . . . so . . . frontally," [Paul] said. "God will let you experience his love, but this is never to be desired. That would be prideful. In fact, it can be harmful to approach God so adamantly. Rather, I think," he said, in a voice of tentative innocence, not that of an expert who as a monk had sought God for almost sixty years, "the whole idea is to cooperate with the little graces every day brings. God lets you know if you are pleasing him or offending him. Monks seek the supernatural, but that is rooted in the natural, in natural relationships, living within the 'School of Charity.'"[2]

This monk goes on to say that we each have our own "school" in which God teaches us, if we will allow it. And that is the genius of the *Rule* of Benedict and the many monastic groups that follow it. Benedict taught clearly that God is present in everyday life; he speaks to us, teaches us and gives us "little graces" as we serve, pray, seek to love the people around us and try to be faithful to what God is teaching us and where God is leading us. Ordinary life overflows with God's presence, and the disciplines of prayer, service and thankfulness enable us to experience that presence.

We may have a stereotype of monastic life as somehow holier than our everyday life. In one sense, monks and sisters live a very ordinary life with mundane tasks to do. They are not superhuman or even super-spiritual. However, their commitment to prayer and to their vows enables them to live in a way that calls into question many aspects of ordinary life that we take for granted. In this increasingly secular, sexualized and materialistic culture, we can learn much from monastic living to illuminate everyday life outside the monastery.

Stability

The first vow laid out in Benedict's *Rule* is stability. To a monk or sister, it means being committed to stay in this particular monastic house with these particular people. It means being willing to look for God here in the constancy of this place in this rhythm of life, rather than seeking God in ever-changing places and varied routines.

Paul Wilkes calls stability a "sense of where you are," and he believes that our disjointed lives and fragmented society present ample evidence that we desperately need to embrace stability. "What was needed, Benedict taught, was maddeningly simple. It was a commitment to trust in God's goodness—that he was indeed there, in that very place; and that holiness, happiness, and human fulfillment were to be found, not tomorrow or over the hill, but here—today."[3]

Wilkes argues that a sense of stability offers a resting place, but that we must not understand stability to mean that we can never change. Because life is a journey, there will always be transitions and changes. Stability, Wilkes believes, "is woven of the ability to stay put and yet never lose the explorer's desire for new experiences. . . . Stability's goal is that we might see the inner truth of who we are and

---

Finding an Anchor

Most of us are not called to the cloister, yet we find the practical common sense of St. Benedict and his commitment to finding the holy in the ordinary readily accessible to us. Even the three monastic vows, stability, conversion of life, obedience, translate readily to life in the world. All of us need an anchor, a place of inner security in the midst of a mobile, transitory world, but as we consent to stability, to being where we are instead of escaping into some temporary bolt-hole, we are called to conversion.

ELIZABETH CANHAM, *Heart Whispers: Benedictine Wisdom for Today*

---

where we are going. That we might be still long enough to be joined intimately to the God who dwells within. . . . It is difficult—no, it is impossible—to find and maintain that center if our waking hours are a blur of mindless activity, without the presence and practice of stability in our lives."[4]

Stability, for those of us not living in the monastic rhythm of prayer services, can mean a commitment to daily, weekly or monthly prayer disciplines. A weekly Sabbath observance and attending church each week can be part of our expression of stability. Faithful demonstrations of family commitments are connected to stability too. Throughout my adult life, I have written to or called my parents every week, and I now understand that rhythm to be part of the structure of stability that keeps me healthy. Faithfulness to our marriage vows, checking in regularly on our neighbors, and consistent attempts to listen to and affirm our coworkers can all be expressions of a commitment to stability, as we realize on a deep level that this is the field where God has planted us and called us to bear fruit.

Benedict calls us to listen as a part of the vow of stability. The *Rule* says, "Listen with the ears of your heart, for the Lord waits for us daily to translate into action, as we should, his holy teachings."[5] We need to listen to the Scriptures in order to know God's teaching. We need to listen to the Holy Spirit, who will teach us how to apply God's truth. We need to listen to our own lives, so we can understand the ways God is speaking to us in this day, in this place.

Retreat director Elizabeth Canham, in *Heart Whispers: Benedictine Wisdom for Today*, talks about the fact that so often when we feel any pain, we immediately choose the appropriate medication to ease it. Sometimes, she believes, God speaks to us through our fatigues and headaches and muscle aches, revealing to us the lack of balance and health in our lives. If we immediately medicate ourselves with drugs or caffeine, we lose the opportunity to hear God speak.[6] We need to learn to listen more deeply even to the negative and irritating things in our daily lives in order to hear God speak to us through every part of daily living.

Canham also points out that the willingness to wait is a part of the vow of stability. Waiting, she says, is difficult for us because "it reminds us that we have not yet arrived, that we are unfinished." Waiting frequently compounds our fears and doubts. Canham believes that we must embrace waiting, in part because "waiting is also God-like. Scripture bears witness to the God who waits again and again for the right moment to act in the life of a community or an individual. That waiting is especially poignant as God takes flesh in the body of a young woman and becomes subject to the nine months of pregnancy."[7]

Canham notes that often we become discouraged as we wait, wondering if God will ever answer our prayers. She believes that our faith and prayer will grow as we honestly acknowledge the turmoil of inner emotions that we experience when waiting. We will grow in our ability to rest in stability. She notes that the Psalms are full of allusions to waiting, which can encourage us as we learn to wait in hope.

The Benedictine vow of stability can be affirming and encouraging as we enter into the second or third decade in the same marriage, the same job, the same church or the same town. We need to be reminded of the significance in God's eyes of continuity and faithfulness.

Many at midlife are beginning to experience the desire to narrow our expectations after a couple of decades of seemingly unlimited possibilities. We have learned that it simply doesn't work when we try to keep all options open all the time. A few commitments, a few essential disciplines can help us stay where we are and look for God in that place. We don't have to do everything. We can rest in the limited view out the round window of the cupola, because we know that we will actually see the sky more clearly when we see only a special part of it.

Conversion of Life

Benedict's second vow nicely balances the vow of stability. We are called, according to the *Rule*, to embrace conversion of life. While we commit ourselves to look faithfully for God in the places and routines we are committed to, we also must allow God to open us to change and growth.

We often use the word *conversion* to refer to the specific point when a person turns away from the former way of life and turns toward God. Benedict used it differently. Benedict saw "conversion" both as a moment in time when we turn toward God and also as a continual process of growth. He believed that movement toward God may begin with one turning, but it must continue with the many small choices of daily living.

Paul Wilkes defines conversion of life as "a continuing and unsparing assessment and reassessment of one's self and what is important and valuable in life." Benedict, Wilkes writes, "saw conversion as a continuing process, one punctuated with more failures than successes."[8]

Conversion of life involves listening to the people around us and truly hearing what they see in us that needs changing. Conversion of life includes embracing conflict as a way in which God teaches us about the parts of ourselves that need to be changed. It involves honestly facing our own faults that hurt others, and constantly turning to God for healing and forgiveness.

Esther de Waal, in *Living with Contradiction: An Introduction to Benedictine Spirituality,* affirms the value of Benedict's "very simple message that we all need to hear: being committed to God is not about being nice. It is about being real."[9] Conversion of life calls us to rigorous self-honesty, which involves a humility and openness that listen hard to the people around us as they help us see ourselves more clearly. The same humility and openness enable us to listen to God.

De Waal points out the amazing balance in Benedictine spirituality between time in community and time spent alone. Monks and sisters in most orders work and worship in community, yet also spend time each day in the discipline of private meditation on Scripture. The daily prayer services also provide a healthy balance of communal prayer and time to reflect. The services involve the singing and reading of lots of Scripture, particularly the Psalms. The repetition of psalms, week in and week out, provides a rhythm that allows for personal reflection during the daily services. The variety of emotions presented in the Psalms also encourages personal honesty.

Several writers on Benedictine spirituality liken the repetition of the psalms in the liturgy of the hours to the waves on a beach, a constant background rhythm that encourages people to go deeper inside their own thoughts, bathed in the presence of God. Conversion of life is simply not possible without reflection and prayer.

Being open to inward repentance, growth and change while being faithful in this place with these people . . . that's the balance provided by the partner vows of stability and conversion of life. Many at midlife articulate that same challenge, perhaps using different words, but facing the same issues: "How can I grow and develop as a person in the midst of all the commitments of my life? I've got a house, a family, a job, a dog, a garden and aging parents. Yet I want to go deeper in my faith. I want to find more meaning and significance in my faith. Can I do that?" Benedict would answer, "Yes, you can."

In order to experience conversion of life at midlife, we must first believe that God desires that we grow and develop throughout our life, in all stages, even if we feel inundated with responsibilities and commitments. We must place sufficient emphasis on conversion of life to make time for at least some of the aspects of the balanced life that Benedict recommends: prayer, work, study and rest. We must understand that growth will certainly be challenging and may even be painful. We will have to let go of our culture's emphasis that everything should be easy. At midlife, more than ever, as we long for meaning, we will have to understand that meaning doesn't come without some degree of discipline. Benedict's third vow, obedience, helps us understand some of the discipline required.

Obedience

We saw the significant role listening plays in fulfilling the vow of stability: God calls us to listen to his voice in this place and in the midst of these commitments. Similarly, we cannot embrace conversion of life without listening to God's leading. Listening is also at the center of the third vow, the vow of obedience.

We may think that a monk or a nun has a commitment to obedience that is totally different from ours because they are called to obey the instructions of the head of their monastery. What lies behind their obedience to the abbess or abbot is a very simple understanding of the call of all Christians to obey God. Christ was obedient unto death, and we are called to be transformed daily into Christ's likeness. Obedience is therefore central to the Christian journey.

Esther de Waal writes that that obedience is about listening, responding and acting on what we hear. Obedience, she believes, is no more than listening to God—and listening is after all the way in which the *Rule* opens. Listen is the very first word of the *Rule*: listening in its fullest sense, listening with every fibre of my being; listening in all the ways in which God is trying to reach me. This will not only be in words (though a dialogue with God through the scriptures, through daily reading, and particularly through the psalms, is very central to Benedictine life). But also listening through the people whose lives touch mine; through the things I touch and handle; through moments of grace. Do I really take this as seriously as I should? Do I not in fact so often take for granted God's amazing generosity?[10]

Elizabeth Canham also stresses the connection between listening and obedience: "The kind of listening Benedict calls for is a deep hearing that moves beyond understanding with the mind to a willingness for the heart to be moved. Because ear and heart are inextricably connected, obedience to God's call follows."[11] She also observes, "We do not readily embrace obedience, and we often expend a great deal of energy in attempts to avoid doing what is required of us. Obedience is hard work (Saint Benedict calls it labor), for it demands of us a searching honesty about our willfulness and challenges our claims of independence."[12]

What does this kind of obedience look like in practice? It includes faithfulness to commitments and thankfulness for God's generosity. It may involve hearing God's call in small things, such as making a phone call to someone experiencing a loss or apologizing for something relatively trivial but potentially hurtful. Obedience may involve a significant life change, such as moving across the country to take a new job or caring for a relative in a costly way.

When we talk about obedience, we must be careful not to put too much emphasis on our own efforts to obey. We are being transformed into Christ's image, and it is Christ in us—through the Holy Spirit—who will enable us to obey. Listening to God for guidance, resting in the power of the Spirit, relying on God to help us obey as Christ did will all be essential as we strive to fulfill the vow of obedience.

For baby boomers at midlife, the vow of obedience may be the most foreign of the Benedictine vows. We can understand God's call to stability, to look for God here in the midst of these commitments. We can understand God's call to conversion of life because

---

God Is Our Active Partner

Too many of us have been raised with an image of God as some sort of celestial bookkeeper, tallying up our many bad deeds and recording the few good ones. Or we see God as some kind of absentee landlord, sending our souls down to take up residence in a body, letting us swing in the wind for a certain number of years, and then swooping back down to reclaim what is his. It takes no great theological or biblical scholar to realize how misleading our images of God can be. God is with us throughout our lives, an active partner. This is spoken of in the Psalms, assured in the Gospels, confirmed in the writing of great mystics, and continually reflected in the lives of people we have known and admired for their steadfast confidence in a power greater than their own. How could we have thought differently?

PAUL WILKES, *Beyond the Walls: Monastic Wisdom for Everyday Life*

---

we generally embrace growth toward wholeness. But obedience calls for a kind of submission that may feel foreign to the "Me Generation."

Esther de Waal points out that all three of Benedict's vows help us to be human but also help us to orient our lives away from ourselves, "away from that subtle temptation of self-fascination and self-discovery. They challenge any spirituality from becoming yet one more expression of the contemporary obsession with the self, with self-awareness, with self-fulfilment. Instead they point me to Christ. Christ the Rock on which I build, Christ the Way I follow, Christ the Word I hear. If I am to put Christ at the centre, as St. Benedict would have me to, that then displaces me from the centre."[13]

De Waal goes on to say that even in the context of the Christian faith, we so often put ourselves at the center, focusing on our own obedience and faithfulness, how well we are serving God, whether or not we are being "good," how much we are attempting to please God. If we truly begin to put Christ's love at the center, then we can live in a receptive stance, ready to receive love as well as guidance about what to do.

The Benedictine viewpoint sees listening and obedience as a part of an interplay between God and humans. This kind of obedience does not involve effort or strain on our part to be good or to do the right thing. Obedience flows out of communication and relationship. Even more significantly, obedience is the fruit of receiving God's love.

As we long for significance and meaning at midlife, Benedict's priorities can help us see that true significance and meaning come from putting Christ at the center, rather than keeping ourselves there. For baby boomers, our generational culture strongly encourages us to focus on ourselves; Benedict teaches us that, in reality, life and health come from focusing on God.

Hospitality, Service and Work

As Brian pointed out in his story at the beginning of the chapter, work and prayer are linked in monastic life in a compelling way. Benedict, with his very practical view of life, saw clearly that most people find it very difficult to pray all day long. Work is the best way to fill the time when not praying. And yet work is more than something to fill time or make money; work is the fruit of prayer, a sacrifice to God and a way to make Christ known in the world.

How greatly this view of work differs from the view that predominates in Western culture! Our culture encourages us to believe that our value and worth lie in our work. We are urged by our culture to a kind of franticness about work; more is always better, and it takes a concerted effort to push toward ever-increasing productivity.

Writing about monastic living in her book *Cloister Walk*, Kathleen Norris notes that "in our culture, time can seem like an enemy: it chews us up and spits us out with appalling ease. But the monastic perspective welcomes time as a gift from God, and seeks to put it to good use rather than allowing us to be used up by it."[14] The peaceful attitude toward work described by so many when they visit monasteries flows out of the monastic sense of time: if God calls us to do something, there will be enough time to do it, because God is the Lord of time. This perspective feels like cool water in a desert land for those people at midlife who are overwhelmed, overworked and just plain too busy.

Hospitality is one kind of work that most monasteries embrace. Benedict put a high value on hospitality, urging monks and sisters to view strangers as Christ himself coming to stay. Guests are to be received as they are and for who they are. There is no mandate to require guests to participate in any of the monastery's activities. At the same time, there is no interruption of the monastery's rhythm because of the presence of guests.

This style of exercising hospitality again demonstrates the kind of balance that Benedict taught: welcoming people just as they are, while continuing to exercise the personal and communal disciplines that God has set forth. I see a great challenge for my own life in this kind of hospitality. When I try to welcome people into my home or into my life, I often give up too much of myself and my own priorities in the process. I love the challenge of Benedictine hospitality that calls me to a kind of serenity as I open my life to others, all the while keeping hold of the disciplines and patterns God has called me to.

At midlife, hospitality can take on increased significance, as we realize how precious are our times with family and friends. In addition, as we realize that many of our blessings are not shared by others, we can grow in extending hospitality to those who cannot recipro-cate. In the midst of the frantic, overscheduled days that are so common during the midlife years, a commitment to hospitality can be difficult to embrace. Yet the simplicity of a conversation over a meal

---

My Possessions Are on Loan

If I try to follow St. Benedict I find that I have to think about the material things in my life, and that I am being called to establish a right relationship with all my possessions. I see myself as a steward, holding these things in trust, enjoying but not owning them. I find this easier to accept in theory than in practice. But when I do remind myself that all these good things belong to God and not to me, I find that my sense of gratitude for the extraordinary generosity of God brings with it also a sense of freedom. All things are on loan, all things come from God, and that includes my own body as well. I have no rights and I do not possess.

ESTHER DE WAAL, *Living with Contradiction: An Introduction to Benedictine Spirituality*

---

continues to be attractive and can help us connect with values that come from deep inside our hearts and souls. (And when this is our goal, a soup-and-rolls meal can often fill the bill better than an elaborate dinner.)

Balance and Paradox

Esther de Waal uses the language of paradox and contradiction to describe Benedict's genius as he interprets the Gospel of Jesus Christ into everyday life. We are called to find God in this place and to seek the peace and discipline of stability, yet we are also called to grow and change and be willing to move. We are called to welcome strangers and accept them for who they are, yet we are not called to change our own priorities as we welcome them.

Many, including de Waal, use the word *balance* to describe the life patterns laid out by Benedict. We are called to prayer, work, study and rest in fairly equal proportions. Each is important, but to overemphasize any one of them would be unhealthy. Benedict invites us to embrace the balance between community, where we live and work, and time alone for prayer and reflection. He encourages us to engage in self-reflection without self-absorption and to strive for sincere repentance without dwelling excessively on our shortcomings.

Benedict calls us to a radical obedience that sees all of life as a response to God's voice and God's initiative, yet we are not urged to strain for that kind of obedience. In fact, Benedict encourages us to accept that we will fail as often as we succeed. We are called to believe that we have enough today, in this moment, while we also acknowledge that we are looking to heaven for our ultimate fulfillment. The grace of God overflows in every moment, in every place and in every human life, and Benedict's balance is firmly rooted in God's character and God's presence with us.

It is not surprising that so many people are finding joy and peace in visiting monasteries to pray and reflect on their lives. Many are choosing to be oblates, people who have made a commitment to be associated with a monastery without becoming monks or sisters. Benedict's wisdom about a balanced life can give us restored perspective for our daily lives. His call to balance is particularly appropriate at midlife, when we realize we need to reevaluate all our scattered priorities and settle into a few disciplines that can serve us into the second half of life.

Those who are unable to visit a monastery may wonder how they can benefit from the Benedictine tradition. More churches and retreat centers are offering day-long prayer retreats, which can be a good way to start. An hour spent alone in an empty church can provide a small taste of the silence and reflection that visitors to a monastery are able to experience.

The call to rhythm that is so much a part of monastic life can flow into our everyday lives if we are intentional. We can adopt habits of prayer that are connected to the events of our lives that happen every day. We can embrace the discipline of praying every day right after the kids leave for school, while we are waiting for the computer to boot up every morning, or when we get in the car to head home at the end of the day. We can read a psalm every night at bedtime.

As I have gotten older, I have come to appreciate praying before meals and before bedtime. When I was younger, I viewed "saying grace" as a perfunctory, legalistic pattern of behavior. Because life has speeded up with each passing year, making moments of prayer requires more discipline, and because I have grown in appreciating the riches that rhythms can give us, I am now deeply grateful for my husband's commitment to pray before meals and before going to sleep.

We can also look at our weekly schedules with regard to Benedict's call to a life of prayer, work and rest with a balance of solitude and community. The three vows—stability, conversion of life and obedience—are very relevant to daily life. Any Bible study group or support group can use Benedict's priorities as a structure for holding each other accountable. At midlife, in the swirl of seemingly endless activities, the balance inherent in Benedict's priorities and vows can help us slow down and find the meaning and depth we long for.

Maureen's Story

Maureen is 45 years old. She speaks at retreats, serves as a spiritual director for several individuals and frequently teaches at her church. Twice she has spent several days at a monastery.

*   *   *

It makes sense that I was around 40 when I first went to stay at a monastery. I was ready to explore God in new ways, not just through the mind. The time at the monastery helped me experience God in ways that were less cerebral, less focused on ideas about God, more focused on the ordinary stuff of life, the rhythms of work, play, and prayer. I experienced the rhythms of God's care in everyday life.

On one of my trips to the monastery, someone I knew was there.

It was the daughter of an old college friend of mine. I never expected to see her there. At the time, I was wrestling with midlife issues. This young woman was the same age as her mother was when I knew her mother. Her presence there enabled me to confront aging in a way I wouldn't otherwise have done.

When I go to a Benedictine abbey, I enter into something that is already happening. I don't have to make it happen. The Scriptures in the prayer services are there for me without effort on my part, and there is often a connection between the Scriptures in the services and the issues God is speaking to me about. Often in my everyday life I feel guilty for not praying enough, but at the monastery it's built in. There's a real freedom to it.

The rhythm of the schedule at the monastery is comfortable for me in decompressing. It takes a while to get into the rhythm of the divine office—the prayer services—but I slowly begin to enter in.

The monks' offer of extended hospitality is a true gift, allowing us to enter into a different pace and a different rhythm for a time, a rhythm based on God's presence in everything.

It's the pictures from the monastery that I hold on to. I can remember watching a monk mowing the grass in the middle of the track where I would run for exercise. He's using one of those riding lawn mowers, and he goes slowly, stopping often to empty the container that holds the cut grass. He shows no hurry whatsoever. He works until the bell rings for prayer, and then he stops. He doesn't work until the job is finished. It was such a contrast with the pace of my running. You really can't get too compulsive about your work if you're going to get interrupted over and over all day by the prayer services.

* * *

Questions for Reflection

To think about, write about or talk about with friends.

1. Consider the three monastic vows—stability, conversion of life,

and obedience. What do they mean to you? What emotions do you feel when you think about each one? In what ways do you already embrace aspects of these vows? In what ways would you like to?

2. Think about the balanced life in a monastery, with an emphasis on work, prayer and rest. In what ways is your life out of balance? What changes would you like to make? Take your desires to God in prayer.

3. If the monastic experience intrigues you, do some research about monasteries located close to you and consider making a visit. Before you go, be sure to think about your expectations and ask someone to pray for you while you are there.

For Further Reading

Elizabeth J. Canham. *Heart Whispers: Benedictine Wisdom for Today.* Nashville: Upper Room, 1999.

Esther de Waal. *Living with Contradiction: An Introduction to Benedictine Spirituality.* Harrisburg, Penn.: Morehouse, 1989, 1997.

Kathleen Norris. *The Cloister Walk.* New York: Riverhead, 1996.

Paul Wilkes. *Beyond the Walls: Monastic Wisdom for Everyday Life.* New York: Doubleday, 1999.

7

Soul Nurture
Drawing Near to God with the Heart

The midlife journey often involves a drive to integrate all the parts of our lives into one whole. As we reach our late thirties or early forties, and as we look back on the first half of our lives, we can see diverse threads, some of them meaningful and some of them trivial and inconsequential. Some of the aspects of our work, some of the things we do for recreation (including that mindless TV show we watch just out of habit), some of the people we spend time with, and some of the habits we have clung to for years seem ridiculously meaningless. We wonder why we have continued to do them. But mixed in with these increasingly unimportant parts of our lives, we find threads that we know are deeply significant to us.

Our culture drives us toward fragmentation, which is coupled in early adulthood with the desire to try lots of things and experiment with many different options. At midlife, people often long to pull out the insignificant threads and find a unifying center for the threads that have meaning but feel dislocated and scattered.

Many describe this process as a move from the head to the heart. We have the sense that in early adulthood we strove to understand the world with our minds, and our minds generated all those enticing possibilities that took us in a variety of directions. At midlife, many experience a desire to live more from the heart, to center our lives more on things that have meaning, to embrace our values with our whole selves, to draw near to God in a way that involves our whole being, our hearts as well as our minds.

Some describe this process as finding and nurturing our soul. In Thomas Moore's *Care of the Soul*, he writes that it is impossible to define the soul in a precise manner, but "we know intuitively that soul has to do with genuineness and depth. . . . Soul is revealed in attachment, love, and community, as well as in retreat on behalf of inner communing and intimacy."[1]

Inner communing, intimacy, attachment to heart values, integration of all the parts of ourselves, being centered . . . these are some of the most encouraging and meaningful aspects of midlife growth and development. Pulled together under the title of this chapter, "Soul Nurture: Drawing Near to God with the Heart," are a variety of emphases that can help us live the whole of our lives in integrity and genuineness. We have seen glimpses of these ideas in the other chapters of this book.

We have seen the way that many at midlife experience God's presence in nature in a sensory way that draws them in a profound way to both worship and creativity. We have seen in Sabbath-keeping an integration of God's call to service with God's call to live simply as a creature dependent on God's grace. We have seen the utter simplicity of the Benedictine pattern of a few significant disciplines. We have seen the attraction of Celtic Christian spirituality, where God's presence is experienced in all of life, and all the diverse bits and pieces of life are integrated into one whole. All of these are part of the experience of God's call to experience him with our hearts, our souls, our whole being. In this chapter we will focus further on these topics.

Many people at midlife report that tears are much closer to the surface than they have ever been before. This is certainly true for me. These are not simply tears of pain; they may also be tears that connect us with profound realities beyond our comprehension, such as the enormity of evil in the world, the great love of God, the great mystery of life, the enormous privilege of loving and being loved. Tears can help us integrate the diverse emotions we experience, and they can help us see what is in our hearts.

Many people at midlife experience God's presence through the arts in a new and noncognitive way. God's presence in daily life through the Holy Spirit may become more vivid. Maintaining or rediscovering old friendships can play a part in unifying our past with our present. Honesty in facing powerful negative emotions and searing, painful memories can help us unify our public persona with our inner self. All the emotions expressed in the Psalms seem more real and more immediate.

Some of these issues can be seen in Don's story.

Don's Story

Don, 54, is a dentist who reduced his work hours at 51 and has taken on more volunteer commitments.

* * *

I became a Christian through InterVarsity Christian Fellowship when I was a graduate student. InterVarsity got me into studying Scripture, to see what's really there, to be grounded in the Word. I still love to study the Bible and underline parts of it.

Now, I find I also like to spend time thinking about Scripture and singing Scripture songs. I like to let Scripture speak to me and question me, rather than me being the one who asks all the questions. Scripture brings out confession because I know how short I fall. I enjoy contemplative prayer in groups, waiting on God rather than just studying about God.

When I go for walks, I enjoy just being able to stop and smell roses, to look up close at flowers and experience them. I like to stop and observe things, small details. Recently we walked in a park with lots of roses. We were surrounded by them, and it felt like heaven. In my twenties, I would rush by. Experiencing God's goodness in daily life is more real to me now.

I'm getting comfortable with the side of me that is sensitive and likes to experience things. I've noticed I cry more easily. I cry in movies, in worship, and particularly during praise songs. Sometimes the worship service is over, and I have tears streaming down my face, and I'm embarrassed as I turn to talk to the people next to me. I can't control it, but I'm learning to be less embarrassed by it as I accept that part of me.

When you're young, you're always looking ahead to being older when things will be better. Or you take for granted that good things will happen again, but they rarely do. I didn't reflect then on how precious certain things are.

My father's death a few years ago affected me a lot. I was with him when he died, and it was like he was teaching me how to die. It was his last lesson for me. Death no longer has its sting. I've been afraid of death all my life. But now I've been with death. I find I want to talk about heaven more, to focus on eternal things, things that are unseen. All this we see is going to turn to dust.

The summer my father died, he showed me all his old blueprints from his job as an engineer. This is the television van he designed, with the camera mounting. He was retired then, and I think he knew he was dying. Those blueprints put my own work into perspective.

Someday someone will clear out all my stuff. This freed me not to be so obsessed with my work, not to take it so seriously.

I realize how short my time is on earth, so I find myself savoring what I experience. It lifts me up to the Lord and gives me a longing for heaven where our experience of God will be much more direct and vivid. I find myself saying, "Thank you that I experience this air, this smell." Since I know my death is approaching, I try to savor this world. My senses are more focused now, and I long for God in a way I never experienced before.

* * *

God Woos Us

Two men at midlife, Brent Curtis and John Eldredge, wrote a fascinating book that develops the idea that God calls us to draw near to him with our hearts. The book's title, *The Sacred Romance: Drawing Closer to the Heart of God*, expresses their conviction that God tenderly woos us and romances us. They believe that if we are not responding to God with our hearts, we are missing something central to the gospel of Jesus Christ:

> In the end, it doesn't matter how well we have performed or what we have accomplished—a life without heart is not worth living. For out of this wellspring of our soul flows all true caring and all meaningful work, all real worship and all sacrifice. Our faith, hope, and love issue from this fount, as well. Because it is in our heart that we first hear the voice of God and it is in the heart that we come to know him and learn to live in his love.[2]

Curtis and Eldredge believe that we easily become preoccupied with "shoulds" and "oughts" and with external concerns like good works, and thus we often center our lives around activity for God rather than focusing on communion with God. We so easily spend energy on the management of our lives rather than addressing questions of meaning and values. They state, "Busyness substitutes for meaning, efficiency substitutes for creativity, and functional relationships substitute for love."[3]

Many at midlife experience a drive to turn inward and discover, or rediscover, the riches of the inner life. Curtis and Eldredge write, "The inner life, the story of our heart, is the life of the deep places within us, our passions and dreams, our fears and our deepest wounds. . . . The heart does not respond to principles and programs; it seeks not efficiency but passion. Art, poetry, beauty, mystery, ecstasy: These are what rouse the heart."[4]

If we want to communicate with our hearts, we must adopt this language of "art, poetry, beauty, mystery and ecstasy." We simply cannot continue to focus only on the outer life of tasks that need to be done and plans that need to be made. We have to devote time and energy to nurturing the things that inflame our souls with passion and lift our hearts to God.

The praise singing that has become so common in many congregations provides a way for people to open themselves to God and bring their whole being into God's presence. Recently I read an article in a Christian magazine by someone who loves hymns and classical music. She dislikes the simplicity, even banality, of many praise songs, but she has reluctantly come to acknowledge that during the praise singing at church she is able to pray in a way that is integrated and very profound. There is something about repeating simple words and a simple tune that frees our heart and soul to enter into God's presence

Curtis and Eldredge discuss the power of stories to help us access our hearts. Jesus was the ultimate storyteller. The parables and incidents recounted in the Gospels contain immense challenge for people at midlife who want to develop their inner lives. The Gospel stories are simple, but they are not easy to understand. Instead they are enigmatic and subtle, just the right kind of literature to help us engage our hearts and souls in order to explore what we really value and what is really important to us, in the light of Jesus' priorities and values. The Gospel stories engage the heart as well as the mind.

In *The Sacred Romance*, the authors discuss the significance of a healthy understanding of heaven. If we live as if this world is all there is, they write, we will place a burden on our experience here on earth that this world was never intended to bear. We will continually try to find heaven on earth, which is impossible, and "we will live as desperate, demanding, and eventually despairing men and women."[5]

Instead, if we can understand and rejoice in the truth that one day God will make all things whole, and that we will live in heaven in

---

Longing for God

As a deer longs for flowing streams,
*   so my soul longs for you, O God.*
My soul thirsts for God,
*   for the living God.*
When shall I come and behold the face of God?
My tears have been my food
*   day and night,*
while people say to me continually,
*   "Where is your God?" (Ps 42:1-3)*

---

unblemished joy and contentment in God's presence, our lives on earth will be transformed. This life is definitely *not* as good as it gets. The best is yet to come.

Mercifully, we get glimpses of heaven in this life. Imagine that a wonderful party is happening nearby, with the most luscious music in the world, and every now and then a bit of music escapes from the party and we get to enjoy it. In the same way, glimpses of heaven permeate our lives on earth. It takes time and effort and being present in each moment for us to be able to notice those glimpses, but the glimpses are worth any effort. They illuminate our lives and gladden our hearts.

Longing for God

Glimpses of heaven, when we can receive them and rest in them, nourish the heart and soul. Those moments of clear vision and certainty lift us up to God and illumine our daily lives. Seeking those glimpses is a worthy endeavor. We rejoice when our seeking brings us what we long for. We also need to grow in acknowledging that our lives on earth will be characterized much more by seeking than by finding.

In *The Awakened Heart*, Gerald May discusses the seeking and longing that characterize our lives. "Emptiness, yearning, incompleteness: these unpleasant words hold a hope for incomprehensible beauty. It is precisely in these seemingly abhorrent qualities of ourselves—qualities that we spend most of our time trying to fix or deny—that the very thing we most long for can be found: hope for the human spirit, freedom for love. This is a secret known by those who have had the courage to face their own emptiness."[6]

Gerald May writes that we are able to fall in love with life and enjoy each day when we learn to befriend our yearning rather than try to avoid it, when we enter into the "spaciousness of our emptiness"[7] rather than trying constantly to fill it up. This is easier said than done, but many at midlife have described a kind of contentedness and peace that comes in accepting life as it is and looking for God's presence in daily life, rather than constantly expecting God to make everything easy and nice.

C. S. Lewis describes the "lifelong nostalgia, our longing to be reunited with something in the universe from which we now feel cut off."[8] He believed this longing is one of the best things about our pilgrim state. In Lewis's autobiography, *Surprised by Joy*, he uses the word *joy* to describe the piercing longing, both bitter and sweet, that we experience when we remember a vivid memory or catch a brief glimpse of heaven. This kind of joy is distinct from pleasure or happiness, and it taps into the emptiness and spaciousness that Gerald May describes.

Lewis's friend J. R. R. Tolkien explained this kind of joy as "a sudden and miraculous grace . . . beyond the walls of the world, poignant as grief."[9] This joy is inextricably connected with our longing for heaven and our realization that this life is not all there is. Lewis reassures us:

> At present we are on the outside of the world, the wrong side of the door. We discern the freshness and purity of morning, but they do not make us fresh and pure. We cannot mingle with the splendours we see. But all the leaves of the New Testament are rustling with the rumour that it will not always be so. Some day, God willing, we shall get in.[10]

Lewis believed that our sense of exile is inseparable from our perception of beauty, which emphasizes again the significance of art, music, poetry and all things that minister beauty to our hearts. As we accept our state of longing, and as we experience glimpses of beauty that remind us of heaven, our hearts will grow soft and receptive to the grace of God.

Unfortunately, in our culture, we are encouraged to fill our longing for freedom, wholeness and joy with countless material objects and endless thrilling experiences: clothing, cars, home furnishings, food, sex, alcohol, drugs, vacations, sports and so forth. Our culture tells us that if we are experiencing desire of any kind, the most important thing to do is fill that desire with something—anything!—immediately. Thus we rush to satisfying our yearnings and cravings without sitting with them long enough to learn from them and to allow them to draw us toward God.

Seminary professor David Rensberger writes, "Although our hunger and thirst are for God, we are always trying to satisfy them with other things. . . . Indeed, our consumer society energetically organizes these means of avoiding the quest for God, offering us a false quest that is sustained with enormous force and skill by the engines of economy, media, and government."[11] Rensberger believes that it requires an equal force and determination to resist our culture and cling to the truth of the gospel that only in God can we find what we long for.

Tears

A few months ago I sat in on one session of a class on the Desert Fathers, those monks of the fourth and fifth centuries who lived in the deserts of Syria and Egypt and who dispensed wisdom to those who came to visit them. I was blessed indeed that this one particular class covered the topic of the Desert Fathers and their attitude toward tears.

The Desert Fathers advocated weeping. They experienced tears as an excellent way to express sadness and sorrow at our own sin. And they believed that when we are crying for our sins, we will find that

---

What Do You Want?

What do you want? Not what do you wish for, what do you fantasize about, what have you added to your list of priorities, but what do you want? What do you long for? What makes your tongue hang out like that of a thirsty deer? What is your heart's desire? We don't often inquire that deeply into ourselves, and if we do, we may not listen very closely to the answer. That is because the answer can be frightening. What we want, at the core of our being, often will take us out of the set paths of our lives and those of society. We want the thing that is no thing; we want what cannot be gotten by any effort or kept by any attentiveness or displayed for any admiration. We want God.

DAVID RENSBERGER, *"Thirsty for God,"* Weavings

---

our tears are also about the joy and wonder of God's grace and forgiveness. These two components of tears, sorrow for sin and joy in God's grace, will not be separate, they believed, but we will switch from one to the other almost instantaneously.

When I became a mother in my late twenties, I was surprised to find how much more easily I cried than ever before. Tears have been closer to the surface for me for twenty years now. But in my forties my tears somehow changed. I couldn't put my finger on the change until that class on the Desert Fathers.

The tears I experience now really are about both sorrow and joy. I do cry about my own sin. These are seldom tears about one-time sins. My tears seem to center on the sins I can't stop doing: recurring negative thoughts about specific people, my tendency to hate myself because of being overweight, and my longings for things I don't have. Just as the Desert Fathers predicted, mingled in with my tears of sorrow for sin I find tears of joy and wonder that God's love is so great and that he has shown that love to me. In fact, it's in the face of God's abundant love and grace that I feel such sorrow, because I can't seem to receive his overflowing love in some parts of my life. I am so blessed, yet I continue to turn away from God's blessings and seek my own way. Not all the time, but more often than I want to. I cry about that.

I also cry about sin in the world. I cry about the 25,000 children who die each day from hunger-related causes, and I cry at the hugeness of evil that keeps the rich and poor so separate and living such different lives. I cry about the hugeness of evil that would motivate people to give their lives so that others would die in a terrorist attack. I cry about the people I know and love at church who are experiencing pain from so many different awful things in their lies. And at the same time I am crying because God's grace and love are much more immense than evil. His love and grace are so real and significant and tangible in so many ways, yet there are so many places in human life that seem immune to his love. How can this be? It makes me cry.

I cry, as well, because of my longing for heaven. I long for the time and place where everything will be made right, where evil will no longer exist, and where my love for God will be able to flower into the kind of joyous obedience and peaceful acceptance that I long for now. I cry because my moments of emptiness now are so painful in the light of the reality that heaven is coming one day.

Sometimes I find myself getting tears in my eyes in a public setting where it is embarrassing to cry. I'm trying to learn to let those tears be there, as an expression of a deep heart-and-soul reality that—mostly— pleases God. As I have accepted my tears more fully, I am finding I can identify more clearly the emotions that lie behind them. Mixed in with the tears that please God—sorrow for sin, the awareness of God's grace, the longing that everything will be put right—are also tears of self-pity and self-aggrandizement. Even in my tears I find the bizarre mix of faithfulness and selfishness that characterizes all of human life— this mix that got me started crying in the first place!

At the beginning of this chapter we heard from Don, who says that he notices how much more easily he cries than he used to. Don is typical of many midlife men and women who find tears much closer to the surface. I commend to you tears as a way of expressing deep longings and heart realities. Our tears can be a tutor to help us under- stand what we are truly feeling and what we truly value. In our tears the Holy Spirit brings out heart realities too deep for words. When we are consumed by embarrassment at our tears, we lose the oppor- tunity to let our tears teach us as they express inner realities without words.

God's Presence Through the Holy Spirit

Many people at midlife have mentioned their new appreciation for the daily guidance of the Holy Spirit. They have grown, they tell me, in their ability to hear the nudging and prompting of the Spirit, and they have grown in their willingness to follow what they hear. They have come to realize that God knows much better than we do what needs to be done in the world.

On the night he was betrayed, Jesus told his disciples that the Holy Spirit "will guide you into all the truth" (Jn 16:13). After the resurrection, Jesus told the disciples to stay in Jerusalem "until you have been clothed with power from on high" (Lk 24:49) by the com- ing of the Holy Spirit. The work of the Spirit in us, leading into truth and giving us the power to obey, becomes more precious than ever before for many at midlife.

For me, most of the Holy Spirit's promptings involve people I need to contact or pray for. "Make that call now," I seem to hear quite often, and I will find the person at home, needing to talk or wanting to share a prayer request. Often I am right in the middle of something else when I feel nudged to act. It's an interruption in my life. But time after time good fruit results from my obedience. I believe that each time I hear the voice of the Spirit and obey, I am training my soul and spirit in a kind of responsive living that can only result in good things for me and for others.

This responsiveness to the Spirit can bring about a spirit of rest and peace, as we realize more deeply that our lives are in God's hands

---

Experiencing God in the Midst of Daily Life

"In my very early years as a Christian, when I was in high school, I was connected with God in a genuine experiential way. But I quickly moved into theology and Bible study, focusing on knowledge and an objectified sense of faith. There was a small emotional part of faith, but it was disconnected to the analytical part. My brother died eight years ago, and that began a process of change. In the past year or so, I'm finally understanding who Christ is and what it's all about. As humans we suffer. My early experience of Christianity was an upward journey to a higher place. Now it feels to me that the core of the message is that in the experience of pain, God brings redemption and comfort. The direction I'm headed is to experience God in the midst of my daily life, in creative activities, in pain and sorrow."

BILL, *age 35*

---

and that God is guiding us each moment. We don't have to strain to obey a set of distant and stringent rules. God calls us gently to obedience as a part of a tender relationship with him. We don't have to rush around, frantically filling our lives with meaningless possessions and thrilling experiences. There is nothing as thrilling as being in the right place at the right time to help someone, and to know that we are there because we listened to the voice of the Holy Spirit speaking into our daily lives.

We often feel we should be working extremely hard, straining to serve God and make a difference in the world; in contrast, this dependence on the Holy Spirit can lead us into a very different style of service and ministry. Instead of feeling like we have to dream up ways to serve God and then execute our ideas with our own energy and perseverance, we can trust that God, through his Spirit, will show us where he is working and where he wants us to be a part of what he is already doing. This view of ministry can free us from pressure to perform and enable us to rest in God as we try to serve him.

This reliance on the Holy Spirit plays a significant part in our desire to bring our hearts before God and know God deep in our souls. It is the Spirit who illuminates our hearts with God's wisdom and values, guiding us "into all the truth" as Jesus promised (Jn 16:13). The Spirit brings the love of God to our inner being. The Spirit guides us in our inner journey, and the Spirit calls us to intimacy and community. Without the Spirit, we cannot experience the passionate wooing of God, and we cannot know how tenderly God longs for us to bring our whole selves to him in integrity and genuineness.

Facing the Inner Darkness

We saw in chapter one the common midlife experience of increasing honesty about the powerful and dark forces at work inside of us that draw us away from God and from what we know to be good. In our early adulthood, we can often fool ourselves into the illusion that we are pretty wonderful people, free of irrational anger, vindictiveness, all-encompassing fear and petty desires. But then, at midlife many find that all sorts of ugly emotions arise. It is no longer possible to hide the truth from ourselves. We truly do have a lot of ugliness inside us. We realize the complexity of our inner emotions: rejoicing and content in God's grace one moment, irritable and unpleasant the next.

At midlife, many of us face our addictive behavior with new honesty. We begin to see more clearly the various counterproductive ways we have tried to fill the God-shaped vacuum inside us. We know our deepest longing is for God, yet over and over we choose food or shopping or pornography to try to satisfy that longing. Common to the midlife journey are honesty and humility in acknowledging the incredibly inappropriate ways we strive to fill our emptiness.

How can we change? How can we learn to live with our emptiness and longing, when all the cultural voices around us are telling us to hurry up and fill up that hole? Gerald May believes that we need to change the way we view life and come to understand that emptiness is a part of the earthly journey, a part that our culture will do nothing to affirm and everything to negate. For me, the Psalms have been a significant source of help, comfort and reorientation in addressing this issue.

God Knows Us Through and Though

O LORD, you have searched me and known me.
You know when I sit down and when I rise up;
  you discern my thoughts from far away.
You search out my path and my lying down,
  and are acquainted with all my ways.
Even before a word is on my tongue,
  O LORD, you know it completely.
You hem me in, behind and before,
  and lay your hand upon me.
Such knowledge is too wonderful for me;
  it is so high that I cannot attain it.

Where can I go from your spirit?
  Or where can I flee from your presence? (Ps 139:1-7)

The variety of emotions in the Psalms is stunning: praise and thankfulness can transition into sorrow, vindictiveness, discouragement and tears within only a few verses. Throughout the ages, the Psalms have encouraged people to bring all our passions and concerns, and even all our pettiness and irritation, into the presence of God. There is no human emotion that is foreign to God; nothing surprises him. "You have searched me and known me. . . . You discern my thoughts from far away" (Ps 139:1-2).

A Journey with the Psalms

Soon after my fortieth birthday, I found I couldn't read the Bible. All of its ethical and theological truths, which I had been studying consistently for the twenty years I had been a Christian, seemed dry and lifeless. It was as if my soul couldn't bear to take in one more piece of truth. My soul was longing for something to touch my whole being, not just my mind.

As I look back, I can see that it wasn't really a time of spiritual dryness; it was more a time to integrate what I already knew and to bring my whole self to God. At the time, though, it was disconcerting and occasionally scary.

I don't really know how it happened, but one day I read a psalm and found that I could connect with the emotions expressed in it. Maybe I heard a psalm in Sunday worship, and I realized the Psalms could help me find the integration I was longing for. Maybe I picked up a Bible and by a random choice (and God's grace), I read a psalm. However it happened, I read one psalm and felt a connection with the Bible for the first time in months. A few days later, I read another psalm. For the next two or three years, the Psalms were my constant companions, even though I still couldn't connect with anything else in the Bible.

The psalm writers came to feel like friends. I was amazed at the variety of emotions portrayed in the Psalms. The integration of my whole being before God, for which I had been longing, came true for me through the Psalms. The Psalms modeled for me the radical truth that every part of me—the loving, peaceful and devoted self, along with the discouraged, irritable and vindictive self—can be brought to God in prayer. The Psalms nudged me into a new kind of prayer involving my whole self and all my emotions.

The sheer overwhelming praises in so many psalms helps us capture that joy and exuberance in God's presence with us. "O come, let us sing to the LORD; let us make a joyful noise to the rock of our salvation!" (Ps 95:1). "Praise him with trumpet sound, praise him with the lute and harp!" (Ps 150:3). Psalm 107 reminds us of a variety of ways God acts in human history. "Let them thank the LORD for his steadfast love, for his wonderful works to humankind" (Ps 107:31).

Emotions that we consider negative are portrayed just as vividly. Discouragement and depression were very real to the psalm writers. "Save me, O God, for the waters have come up to my neck. I sink in deep mire. . . . I am weary with my crying: my throat is parched" (Ps 69:1-3). The psalmist sometimes felt distant from God: "My eyes grow dim with waiting for my God" (Ps 69:3).

Self-pity, anger, irritation and desire for vengeance all appear in the Psalms. Here is just one example: "One who secretly slanders a neighbor I will destroy" (Ps 101:5). This profound honesty about the vicissitudes of human emotion can be very helpful at midlife, when life often seems more confusing than ever before and when we grow in facing the inner darkness inside us. Longing and thirsting for God are woven throughout the Psalms, and the psalm writers move rapidly from longing to praise and thanks and confession and back to longing. The Psalms validate our spiritual experience in a way that no other literature can do, and they give us hope that our painful longings and uncomfortable yearnings may give way to praise any moment.

In my years with the Psalms, I read them, prayed them, memorized them, sang them, wrote bits of them in my calendar, and allowed them to shape my own prayers. I'm not the same person I was in my thirties, and part of that change was brought about by my immersion for several years in the Psalms. The Psalms have allowed me to face my own inner turmoil more honestly and they have helped me bring more parts of myself to God in prayer. They have called me

---

Facing My Inner Conflicts

The psalms allow me to face my inner conflicts. They allow me to shake my fist at God one moment, and then next to break out into spontaneous song. I am angry, but then I am grateful. I complain at the bitterness of my lot, and then I rejoice at the untold blessings which I receive. If I discover the fullness of my own humanity I also discover the many faces of God. If the story of the people of Israel and their struggle in holding on to the covenant is also my own story, the psalms leave me in no doubt as to the difficulties involved in that relationship. That in itself is consoling. For here is a people who experience struggle and sacrifice, who know the light and the dark, hunger and thirst, who grumble and complain, and who rejoice and praise—and who have no inhibitions in doing this completely openly and vigorously.

ESTHER DE WAAL, *Living with Contradiction*

---

to praise and thanks in a powerfully transforming way. They have given me the kind of hope that resides deep in the heart and illuminates daily life.

Praying the Psalms

Throughout the ages, the Psalms have been the prayer book of the Bible, used by Jews and Christians for individual prayer and for prayer in congregations. At midlife, as we learn to face with increased honesty the wide variety of emotions inside us, praying the psalms can be both comforting and challenging. During my years of psalm reading, I often found that my reading turned into prayer, and I came to love the psalms as prayers. They voice for me so many parts of myself, and they bring those aspects of my personality and emotions into God's presence in prayer.

When I pray the psalms, I receive several gifts from God. I feel connected to people throughout the ages who have prayed these same words. Because so many of my unsettling emotions are expressed in the psalms, I feel that God must accept my volatile and passionate feelings because the psalm writers and so many people down through the years have brought those very same emotions to God in prayer. When I pray the psalms, I receive peace and acceptance from God.

If you want to begin a pattern of praying the psalms, here are some suggestions. If you want to pray a psalm that is completely new to you, or only somewhat familiar, it helps to read the psalm through first to get an idea of what it is about. Then pray it. You may feel most comfortable reading the words very slowly as you pray. I find that when I pray a psalm, I read the words more slowly than usual, but only slightly more slowly. The pace is up to you. Experiment with what seems most comfortable.

You may wonder where to start if you want to begin to pray the psalms. One suggestion is to start with psalms you have read or heard before. Find those familiar psalms in your Bible and, instead of reading them, pray them. Often I start with a well-loved psalm and then continue praying the ones that come next. You can also start at the beginning, with the first psalm, and pray one or more each day. A wide variety of emotions and styles of prayer can be found in almost any set of consecutive psalms.

Often when praying a psalm, I find that the emotions being expressed are not anywhere close to what I am feeling at the time. In those instances, I often find myself remembering other times when I've felt those emotions. I also remember that others all around the world must be feeling those emotions right at the moment I am praying. I try to pray the words on behalf of the people whom God loves who are feeling those emotions right now. In that way, praying the psalms is a prayer form that connects me with people all over the world.

Praying psalms in a group setting is also very rewarding. Invite the group to begin by reading the psalm aloud as a group, either in unison or having one half read the odd numbered verses and the other half read the even numbered verses. Then give the group enough time to pray the psalm individually in silence. After a nice leisurely amount of time, read the psalm aloud again, using the same method as you used the first time. You may want to end with a time of sharing, allowing participants to describe what the experience was like for them. Or you may want to encourage participants to write in a journal after the prayer time.

Penny's Story

Penny, 39, a composer and musician, has experienced a deep change in her experience of God. Her story describes one person's experience of nurturing faith in her heart and soul.

*   *   *

We were in Thailand on vacation. One day we were talking with a Sikh holy man. He was talking about his childhood in a Christian school. He asked me what I thought about religion. I surprised myself when I said, "I think this: religion started in my head and has moved to my heart.

He said, "I understand."

I was raised in a very conservative Christian home, and I grew up being afraid of everything. I've read the Bible for all my life and memorized parts of it. About ten years ago I had a very different experience, more mystical, that overhauled my whole faith and my body. I didn't know at first if anyone else had this mystical experience of faith.

The Celtic saints helped me see that others had the same kind of experiences: the monks in their huts, the birds sitting on their hands, the animals helping them. I read George MacDonald. In Julian of Norwich I found such a sweetness that I had never before experienced. St. Francis has had a big impact on me. Francis had such a connection to the earth. He would move an earthworm off the path. Everything that has life in it is important. I began seeing things through Francis's eyes. He took the bitter for the sweet. He was so humble. I am very vain and materialistic, and I am always humbled when I read his writing.

When faith descends to the heart it becomes more restful. I like the phrase "active resting." It involves letting things happen to you rather than trying to make them happen.

I took a vow about three years ago. I read about the threefold vows monks and nuns take. My vow involved three words: acceptance, thankfulness and love. I needed to accept things for what they were. Then I needed to take a step further and be thankful for them. The third part of the vow was baffling to me; I didn't know why I needed to take it, but I knew I needed to learn about love. Slowly it's opening up to me.

It seems to me that acceptance is resting, receiving. Taking it further into thankfulness brings joy. The outcome is that I experience love for people and for the earth. Love is a kind of uniting factor which ties it all together.

* * *

Drawing Near

In this chapter we have covered a variety of topics that are all connected to the idea of drawing near to God with our heart and soul. I want to make some practical suggestions about how you can integrate these ideas into your life.

Art, music and poetry are gateways to the heart and soul for many people. If that is true for you, you could build on that reality by spending some time on a regular basis journaling or talking with others about what you experience through a favorite piece of art, music or poetry. You may even want to try creating some new or renewed artistic expressions yourself. They don't have to be complex or wonderfully executed; you are not entering a competition. Don't take lightly the role of any and all forms of artistic expression in helping us draw near to God with our whole beings. Be willing to nurture your creative side as a spiritual discipline.

Meditating on heaven can also be very feeding to the soul. If you've never thought much about heaven, you may find you enjoy doing so. Reading the first five and last two chapters of the book of Revelation is a good first step. Meditating about heaven is not some sort of "pie in the sky" exercise; it can help us access some of our deepest longings for the world to be put right and for God's love to permeate all of human life.

Noticing and accepting the emptiness and longing in our lives can also be an important part of honoring God with our heart and soul. Emptiness and unfulfilled longings are a part of human life on earth, and one significant spiritual exercise is to identify what we use to try to fill the emptiness. Journaling or talking with friends about the places of emptiness and longing in our lives can be very helpful in learning to live more peacefully with the reality that in this life we simply won't have everything we long for. God will meet us in our longings in many different ways, but often he doesn't simply hand over to us the thing for which we are longing.

For those who find tears much closer to the surface than they used to be, it will be important to accept tears as a gift. When we let go of embarrassment about the tears, we will be more able to identify what the tears are bringing to the surface from our inner being. Just as the Desert Fathers taught, tears are valued throughout the Bible as an expression of both sorrow and joy. Your tears may very well help you identify and express some of the sources of both sorrow and joy in your life, and thus they will help you live authentically before God, bringing your heart and soul to him.

The Holy Spirit is the one working inside us who enables us to integrate our hearts and souls with the whole of our lives. If you've never spent time considering the work of the Holy Spirit, you will find amazing riches there. John 14—16 is a good place to start, and there are many helpful passages in Acts and the Epistles. It is only because God lives in us through the Holy Spirit that we can look for God's presence in our heart and soul. The Spirit's presence is an amazing gift of grace that enriches our lives immeasurably whether we know it or not. Noticing the Spirit's presence can help us draw near to God with our whole being.

Of course, I always recommend praying the Psalms as a way to draw near to God with authenticity and heart honesty. You may be thinking of other disciplines or practices that help you draw near to God with your heart and soul. Whatever you do, remember that God cares about our inner being as much as he cares about what we do or say or how we live. Our inmost thoughts, feelings and longings are important to him! And he desires to meet us in that inner place we call *heart* or *soul*.

All Will Be Well

In the Psalms we read, "I sought the LORD, and he answered me" (Ps 34:4). God meets us and cares for us and answers our prayers. At the same time, the psalm writer acknowledges, "my tears have been my food day and night" (Ps 42:3). We ache to see God's pure beauty and majesty in the face of this broken world we experience every day. We long to be free from all the seductive desires that sidetrack us so often. We long to see the people we love freed from illness, addictions, pain and suffering.

We live in joy because God loves us, and we can know that love in Jesus Christ. We live in longing and emptiness because sin and death still have so much power. Our hearts are full, and our hearts are broken.

David Rensberger reassures us:

Our thirst for God will be satisfied. Once we have become aware of this yearning, once this passionate need and longing has opened up with us, we can hear a stream off in the distance gurgling toward us. We bend every effort to find that stream. However strong or persistent our efforts, though, they are insignificant compared with the mighty rush of water coming to meet us. Though we may try to slake our thirst elsewhere, the Living Water will find our parched mouths. It will not be our small dippers that finally bring the water to our tongues. Rather, it will be the desire of the Water itself to meet our need, the love of the One whom we have struggled to learn to love, that will overcome our last resistance and pour delicious satisfaction on our aching lips.[12]

Truly Jesus, the giver of Living Water, calls us to bring to him our hearts, our souls, our very beings because he is giving back to us his heart of love.

Questions for Reflection

To think about, write about or talk about with friends.

1. Consider the messages you received in your childhood and teen years about showing emotion, particularly crying. If you cry from time to time now, how do you feel about it? Can you identify some of the emotions that are expressed in your tears?

2. Make a list of the things you long for. Reflect on the ways God has met you in those longings or changed you because of those longings. In what ways do your unfulfilled longings connect you to a longing for heaven? In what ways do you try to meet your longings yourself—and which of those ways are healthy and which have proven to be unhealthy?

3. What do the words *heart* and *soul* mean to you? What place do these words have in your life before God? What place would you like them to have? What relative value do you place on your inner life

of faith in comparison with your outer, visible life of faith? In what ways do you experience God meeting you in your inner life? Spend some time thanking him.

For Further Reading

In the Bible: Psalm 42; 43; 90; 91; 139; John 14—16; Revelation 1—5; 21—22.

Douglas Connelly. *The Promise of Heaven: Discovering Our Eternal Home.* Downers Grove, Ill.: InterVarsity Press, 2000.

Brent Curtis and John Eldredge. *The Sacred Romance: Drawing Closer to the Heart of God.* Nashville: Thomas Nelson, 1997.

Evan Howard. *Praying the Scriptures: A Field Guide for Your Spiritual Journey.* Downers Grove, Ill.: InterVarsity Press, 1999.

Gerald May. *The Awakened Heart.* New York: HarperSanFrancisco, 1991.

Eugene Peterson. *A Long Obedience in the Same Direction: Discipleship in an Instant Society.* Downers Grove, Ill.: InterVarsity Press, 1980, 2000.

8

Listening to God
The Contemplative
Christian Tradition

Throughout the centuries, Christians have valued quiet prayer, reflection on the Scriptures and meditation on the character and purposes of God. In the twentieth century, both in North American culture and in some others, these quiet prayer forms were largely eclipsed by an emphasis on more outwardly oriented expressions of faith.

But lately, more Christians are rediscovering the joys of meeting God in quiet prayer and reflection. Retreat centers offer quiet retreats. Congregations sponsor contemplative prayer events. More Christians visit monasteries to soak up the quiet and peace.

At midlife, paying attention to the inner life and to contemplative prayer can feel more natural than in the first half of life. As we can see from Linda's story, contemplative prayer also addresses several other aspects of midlife faith development.

Linda's Story

Linda is 48 years old and works as an editor. In recent years, she has developed an appreciation for contemplative prayer. Here's the way she describes the significance of contemplative prayer in her life:

*   *   *

I learned about contemplative prayer when I was around 40. It dovetailed perfectly with other things that were going on in my life.

I am an introvert. My mother is extremely extroverted. In recent years, she has developed some ability to pray alone and to appreciate quiet things, but in my childhood and early adult years, her values were totally and completely placed in the realm of activity and socializing. She has a very high energy level, she values action over being quiet, and she has always kept a social schedule that makes me feel exhausted just to hear about it.

In my teen years and early adult years, I strained to be more like my mother. It has only been at midlife that I have begun to accept myself and allow myself to be an introvert. Ironically, people call me energetic. They don't see the hours of quiet that I need to balance outward activity.

I have always valued quiet prayer and reflection, but I felt somewhat guilty for how much I like to be alone with my thoughts and alone with God. This drive to spend time alone made me feel ashamed and inadequate. Learning about contemplative prayer gave validation to these inner drives. In fact, I find contemplative prayer very natural. I'm actually good at something that more outwardly oriented people find difficult. But it took me until midlife to appreciate the strength of my inner life.

The specific prayer styles of contemplative prayer—*examen, lectio divina,* breath prayer and so on—have given me more options for quiet prayer, more things to do as I pray. I love them all. They are very helpful to me.

What is even more helpful is the general attitude that we embrace in contemplative prayer. At midlife I have slowed down, let go of some of my need for control, and tried to live my life more in response to God. In intercessory prayer, which I still value, we say, "Dear Lord, here are the things that are on my mind." And we tell God what we long for and hope for.

In contemplative prayer we say, "Lord, enable me to hear you. What do you want me to pray for? What is in your heart that you want to communicate to me today?" This posture of listening changes the whole focus, and it fits perfectly with what has been going on in my life in my forties.

In my teens and twenties, I really believed I knew a lot, and I was always striving to know more. I felt that I had right answers a lot of the time. Now, in my late forties, I'm so much less certain about lots of things. I still pray lots and lots of intercessory prayers for people in need, for my children and my husband and the things going on in their lives, for the needs of the world. But because I'm less certain about so many things, I really want to be guided in how to pray. I really want to listen to God's concerns, God's priorities, God's passion. I want to hear his voice in how to pray.

In my twenties and thirties, I felt very optimistic that I could do most things that came along, that I would have time and energy to explore what I wanted to. In my forties, I find I have so many relationships, so many options, so much to do. I need guidance and a sense of priorities. I find that guidance through listening to God in contemplative prayer.

And I want to hear his voice of grace, too. All that busy activity of my early adult life came in part from my doubts about who I am and what I do. Now that I'm older, I'm more able to rest in God's love for me, but I need to hear and feel that love. Contemplative prayer encourages me to wait and listen for it.

The specific patterns of prayer that we call contemplative are just a means to an end. And that end is a posture of listening, an attentiveness to the voice of God. I find I can't live without it.

*   *   *

Contemplative Prayer at Midlife

Quiet forms of prayer have always felt natural to Linda, but she was ashamed of her drive to spend time alone with God. Christian "spirituality" has often emphasized service, evangelism, caring for people in need, fellowship and sharing, at the expense of quiet, reflective forms of spirituality. For those of us who find quiet reflection natural, learning about contemplative prayer can be a freeing and joyful midlife experience.

Others find themselves surprised at the comfort and delight they experience in quiet prayer, often for the first time in their lives. In the first half of their lives, they thrived on all the abundant opportunities for fellowship and ministry offered by their churches. They are often surprised in their forties and fifties to find themselves seeking out opportunities to spend time with God in a quiet setting. They are also surprised at how refreshing it feels.

Several extroverted and very social people have told me that at midlife they began to wonder if they really were introverts after all, because they found such joy in being alone and praying alone. Being alone takes on a richness and peace that it never had before. Journaling, creating a prayer space in the home or in the garden, walking alone in nature, and many other forms of prayer and reflection in solitude can take on new meaning and satisfaction as a way to be alone (yet not alone, because God is present).

Linda's story illustrates some of the additional connections between contemplative prayer and midlife growth. In her forties, Linda finds herself relinquishing her need for control. She longs to receive guidance from God regarding her daily life: Who should she spend time with? How should she use her time? What should her priorities be? More than ever before, she desires to live her life in response to God's initiative, and she finds contemplative prayer helps her hear God's voice of direction and his voice of grace.

The Steady Gaze of the Soul

Put simply, the contemplative life is the steady gaze of the soul upon the God who loves us. It is "an intimate sharing between friends," to use the words of Teresa of Avila.

RICHARD FOSTER, *Streams of Living Water*

An Overview of Contemplative Prayer

The long history of contemplative prayer offers quite a few prayer forms that can be very helpful tools. In this chapter we will explore these patterns of prayer:

◆ Breath prayer, a way of stopping and experiencing God's nearness

◆ *Examen,* a way of reflecting back to see God's presence in past moments

◆ *Lectio divina,* a fourfold pattern of sitting with a passage of Scripture

◆ Ignatian prayer, a way to meet Christ by entering into a biblical story

These are very helpful prayer forms to learn, because they give us something to "do," somewhere to direct our thoughts and prayers, as we learn to sit still in God's presence. They are useful skills, and I will write about them in this chapter because they are helpful, rich and rewarding. But the deeper issue that lies behind contemplative prayer, and the goal of using all the skills, is to learn to be present to God and to grow in our ability to hear God's voice, so we can live our lives in response to his presence.

In the first half of life, we can easily delude ourselves that we are competent, in-charge people who can easily know and obey God through our own efforts of discipline. In the midlife years, many people find it difficult to sustain these illusions of control and competence. In addition, we find ourselves longing to know if God is real, if God really can communicate to us, if God really does love us just the way we are. We long to experience God's presence.

Contemplative prayer can give us the space and time in our lives so we can hear God's voice and rest in his presence. As we consider contemplative prayer, we talk about "our presence for God," which focuses on our willingness for God, our openness to God, our commitment to take the time required to hear God's voice and experience God's presence. Contemplative prayer, at its heart, acts out the truth that our lives depend on continual grace from God, poured out upon us. Contemplative prayer allows us to relinquish the myth that it is our discipline or our competence that runs our lives.

As we practice contemplative prayer, this "presence for God" begins to spill over into our everyday lives, and more and more we experience God's hand in daily life. We grow in acknowledging our dependence on God.

Being Alone . . . Perhaps in the Presence of Others

Any contemplative prayer form can be practiced alone. You are warmly invited to experiment with the forms of prayer described in this chapter as you pray by yourself. In addition, you may find great joy in experiencing contemplative prayer in a group.

I can remember the first time, more than ten years ago, that I heard someone describe her experience of silent prayer in a group. She was the pastor of a Presbyterian church located near several other churches. She told me that every Friday all the ministers of the churches, along with anyone else who wanted to come, gathered in the sanctuary of the Episcopal church over lunch hour and they prayed silently together for an hour.

I was incredulous. I didn't say anything out loud to her, but inside I was thinking, *You mean you gather with a group of people for an hour and you don't talk? At all? How weird! You can pray alone at home. When you're with people, what's most fun is to talk. This is craziness!*

Soon after that conversation, I began to attend contemplative prayer events in my own congregation. At first I felt very self-conscious praying silently in a room with other people. After a while, I began to realize it was one of the richest experiences of community that I had ever experienced.

A few years ago, I interviewed participants in one contemplative prayer class for our church newsletter. "What is contemplative prayer like for you?" I asked them. "And why would you encourage others to participate?"

Here are some of the answers: "I like that you have an affinity with people without talking. God is joining hearts together." "I like everyone here. It's a liking that comes out of quiet." "It's a time to be alone with God but without loneliness, because there's intimacy with God and with others." "Being quiet with God enables us to be a group. It begins with our relationship with God and then we can share it with the people around us."

I feel more comfortable now suggesting a period of quiet at the beginning of meetings. Freedom from words is a great gift I am only beginning to understand. I encourage people who want to learn patterns of contemplative prayer to participate in a contemplative prayer group of some kind, because that experience of intimacy in silence with others as well as with God is a great gift.

Breath Prayer

The simplest form of contemplative prayer involves focusing on our breath. Slowing down our breathing has the physiological effect of slowing down all our systems, including our racing minds. Therefore, a brief focus on breathing at the beginning of any prayer time can be very helpful. Breathe slowly and deeply—from the diaphragm rather than from the upper chest—as you begin to pray, and you will often find it easier to relax into God's presence, love and peace.

After the initial slow-down using our breath, we can move onto another form of contemplative prayer, intercessory prayer, a prayer of confession, or any other kind of prayer. Or we may choose to stay with breath prayer for a longer period of time.

God is present in all of creation. "In him we live and move and have our being," says the apostle Paul to the Athenians (Acts 17:28). Through the Holy Spirit, God lives inside all Christians. The air we breathe is a good metaphor to help us understand and experience God's presence around us and in us.

In breath prayer, we focus on our breath: breathing in, breathing out. We focus on our breath as a reminder that at any moment of our lives we can rest in the reality that God's love and care, God's peace and protection, are just as present in our lives as the air is. We rest in the joy of being children who are cared for by a loving and powerful heavenly Father. We rest in the reality that God is in control of the universe and we are not. God really is all around us and even in us, just like air, and we are safe, loved, and protected by his wonderful presence.

During breath prayer, we can imagine that we are breathing in God's Holy Spirit with each indrawn breath, and we can picture ourselves releasing our cares and worries each time we breathe out. Sometimes it takes me many, many breaths before I have released all my cares and worries to God! Some people find it helpful to repeat words as they focus on their breath, such as "Lord Jesus Christ" with the indrawn breath and "Have mercy on me" while breathing out.

Distractions

In any form of contemplative prayer, all sorts of distractions usually crowd into our minds. Even people very experienced in contemplative prayer will often find themselves amazed—and even amused—at the array of distractions the mind brings into focus during prayer. There's nothing wrong or sinful about distractions in prayer. Sometimes the distraction is itself a call to prayer, and a brief intercessory prayer about the situation we're thinking about can help us return to the original intent of the prayer time.

It can also be helpful in coping with distractions to use an image or word picture. Imagine that the random thoughts are like leaves on a tree. In your mind, watch them fall off the tree and be blown away by the wind. Or imagine them floating by on a beautiful stream. You can

---

Watch for the Fruit of Prayer

It is unwise to judge a prayer period on the basis of your psychological experience. Sometimes you may be bombarded with thought all during the time of prayer; yet it could be a very useful period of prayer. Your attention might have been much deeper than it seemed. In any case, you cannot make a valid judgment about how things are going on the basis of a single period of prayer. Instead, you must look for the fruit in your ordinary daily life, after a month or two. If you are becoming more patient with others, more at ease with yourself, if you shout less often or less loudly at the children, feel less hurt if the family complains about your cooking—all these are signs that another set of values is beginning to operate in you.

THOMAS KEATING, *Open Heart, Open Mind*

---

also imagine that your distracting thoughts are like boats on a river. Notice them as they float by. Let them glide away down the river. Resist the temptation to get into one of those boats and rummage around in the hold! But if you do find yourself rummaging around, delving deeply into some problem or issue in your life, notice that it is happening, step back and let that situation float away down the river or drift away in the wind. Return to your original intent in prayer.

There's no need to feel guilty about distractions in prayer. But neither should we encourage them. At every point that we become conscious that we are off track, we can calmly remind ourselves of our original intent and return to it as soon as possible.

Examen: **Gentle, Unforced Noticing**

In the ancient prayer of *examen*, we take time to look back and try to see the hand of God in our lives. *Examen*, like all contemplative prayer forms, is most effective when it is unforced, when we try to let our awareness of God float into our minds rather than forcing ourselves to review every event in an analytical fashion to see if we can detect the presence of God.

First, select a period of time to focus on. It's best to look at one day, although you could also choose to look at a period of a few days or even a week. Focus your thoughts and your heart on the time period you have selected. Ask God to bring to mind one or two times when God was present in your life.

Don't analyze. Don't try to go sequentially through all the events in that time period. Just try to gently notice. In the prayer of *examen*, to notice is to pay attention, to turn your gaze from the present or the future to the past, focusing on the events that took place, the meaning you placed on them and the possibility that God was working in and through what happened.

When you are able to identify one or two times when God was present to you, respond to God in the light of your noticing. You may want to imagine yourself holding in your hand that moment of God's presence, offering it back to God in thanks. You may want to picture yourself smiling at God. You may want to thank God for that moment, using words.

Continue in an atmosphere of noticing. This time, ask God to bring to mind one or two moments when you resisted God's presence. Again, don't try to analyze or examine your life's events sequentially. Try to let a memory of resistance to God float into your conscious mind.

When you are able to identify one or more moments when you resisted God, spend some time responding to God. You may want to pray, "Lord, have mercy." You may want to offer that moment to

God and ask him to heal and transform you. You may want to move into a time of confession of sin.

We so often forget to take the time to notice the patterns of our lives. *Examen* is a lovely discipline because it gives a structure to pay attention to God's working. Often God is present in our lives and we fleetingly experience that presence, but we rush on to the next event and neglect to ponder the patterns of his presence and to thank God for the gift of our awareness of him. *Examen* gives us the opportunity to notice the hand of God, something many midlife folks are longing for.

Examen also gives us the opportunity to notice the patterns of our resistance to God's work in our lives. Sometimes we can change those patterns by conscious discipline. More often all we can do is offer our patterns of resistance to God and ask for his help and mercy. Either way, simply noticing our resistance makes us more likely to notice God's presence next time.

My husband and I have found that the prayer of *examen* has impacted the way we talk to each other at the end of the day. Often my husband will ask me at bedtime, "When did you feel closest to God today?" or "When did you experience God's hand in your life today?" I am always grateful for that question, because it makes me stop and notice.

Examen is a wonderful discipline for midlife. The speed of our lives and the necessity to focus on the future keep us from recognizing when God has been at work in us. Most people at midlife long for meaning and the assurance that life has value. What better way to find meaning and value than to take the time to notice what God is already doing?

A New Approach to the Bible

When we think of reading the Bible, many of us think about how we wish we could take more time for serious Bible study. Many of us were nurtured in our Christian faith through intensive Bible study. In

Bible study groups, we analyzed biblical passages and thought hard about how to apply the passages in our lives. We expected God to speak to us through our study and analysis. Maybe we also memorized verses of Scripture, trying to store God's Word in our heart.

The contemplative approach to the Bible takes these patterns of Bible study a step further. We embrace disciplines that can help us to hear God's voice through the Scriptures.

First and foremost, the contemplative pattern of interacting with the Scriptures is a pattern of meditation on a biblical passage: spending time allowing the Word to sink deep into our souls, letting the truth penetrate our whole being. The groundwork laid by intensive Bible study and Scripture memory can be very helpful as we go a step further, spending time quietly living with a passage of Scripture.

Meditation on the Scriptures has a long history in both Jewish and Christian tradition. In recent centuries, with our emphasis on science and objective truth, we have neglected meditation in favor of analysis and cognitive understanding. Midlife is an excellent time to return to the ancient pattern of meditation upon Scripture. Receptive, quiet reflection on a biblical passage can help us address many of the issues of midlife, enabling us to hear God's voice of guidance and acceptance, helping us let go of the illusion of control, giving us the opportunity to slow down and quiet the many voices that assault us.

The writer of Psalm 1 was well acquainted with this slow, quiet absorption with the Scriptures. Here is a description of those who obey God: "Their delight is in the law of the LORD, and on his law they meditate day and night" (Ps 1:2). Richard Foster writes that examples of the contemplative tradition abound in the Bible, "from the psalmist, who meditated upon God's character, law, and creation, to Mary, the mother of Jesus, who pondered all things in her heart; from Elijah, who kept a lonely vigil over earthquake, wind and fire, to Mary of Bethany, who chose to sit at Jesus' feet."[1]

When we spend time with a passage from the Bible, pondering in our hearts the way God works and asking God to speak to us, we are entering into this long Christian tradition of contemplation and meditation. When we sit at Jesus' feet by reading about him in one of the Gospels and living with that story for a while, expecting Jesus to be present in our thoughts and prayers, we are entering into contemplation and meditation. When we walk through our neighborhood, thinking about a Scripture passage we know by heart or weighing the issues discussed in a recent Bible study, we are engaging in Christian meditation.

All these activities require a commitment to slow down and allow space to ponder the work of God and to listen for God's word to us this day. In our busy and rushed world, making time for reflection will probably be the greatest challenge facing us if we want to move toward contemplative prayer and meditation.

In addition, we may experience the challenge of not knowing how to start. Three longstanding patterns of engagement with the Scriptures can provide a structure for a meditative approach to the Bible: *lectio divina* (sacred reading), Ignatian prayer, and praying the Psalms, which we looked at in chapter seven.

Lectio Divina: **Letting God Speak Through Scripture**

Lectio divina, which simply means "sacred reading" in Latin, is an ancient four-step pattern of reading the Bible and listening for God's word to us. It was developed in the fourth century, so as we use it, we can rejoice in our connection with Christians throughout the ages. The word *sacred* is a great place to start. Just the mention of that word slows me down and makes me expectant that this way of looking at Scripture will enable me to encounter something sacred, something holy.

In *lectio divina* we begin by reading a passage slowly and carefully, not so slowly that we are uncomfortable, but just slowly enough to enjoy observing details in the passage. The passage may be one or two verses, or it may be an entire chapter. As we read, we watch for a word or phrase that jumps off the page at us, a word or phrase that shimmers. In this first step, we engage our powers of observation.

In the second step, we think about the passage, not straining to

---

A Divine Remedy for Our Illness

Contemplative prayer is addressed to the human situation just as it is. It is designed to heal the consequences of the human condition, which is basically the privation of the divine presence. Everyone suffers from this disease. If we accept the fact that we are suffering from a serious pathology, we possess a point of departure for the spiritual journey. The pathology is simply this: we have come to full reflective self-consciousness without experience of God. Because that crucial reassurance is missing, our fragile egos desperately seek other means of shoring up our weaknesses and defending ourselves from the pain of alienation from God and from other people. Contemplative prayer is the divine remedy for this illness.

THOMAS KEATING, *Invitation to Love*

---

analyze it, but peacefully thinking about what the passage means. In this second step, we engage our minds and our thinking process.

In the third step, we respond to God in any way that feels appropriate. We may say a prayer of intercession, confession, praise or thanks. We may simply open our heart to God, imagining our life or some insight gained from the passage held in our open hands, lifted into God's presence. We may visualize Jesus nailed to the cross while we place at his feet the concerns raised by the passage. In this step we engage our hearts, and we bring our emotions into God's presence as we respond to the passage.

In the fourth step, we sit and wait. We may return to the word or phrase that shimmered, asking God to speak to us through that word. In this step, we may receive an image, picture or metaphor from God that seals the significance of the text for us. We may receive a word of love from God. We may just rest for a few moments in the sacredness of God's holiness and love and his presence with us in the world.

We may repeat these four steps over and over in a single passage, stopping in the middle of the first step as soon as we find a word or phrase that shimmers, and moving on to the next three steps, then beginning with the first step again as we continue to read the passage.

The four steps are fluid, not rigid. We may find ourselves jumping from the first step to the third or fourth.

People who are accustomed to rigorous Bible study often describe their pattern of study as "asking questions of the text." In *lectio divina* we allow the Scriptures to ask questions of us. We are not regarding the text with questions in our minds; instead we are allowing the passage to gaze upon us and address us.

Lectio divina is a lovely way to interact with God's Word because it engages our whole beings: our mind and our hearts, our ability to notice details and our propensity to think in images and metaphors. *Lectio divina* enables us to be receptive, encouraging us to believe that God wants to speak to us and that we can receive from God. In *lectio divina*, Bible study and prayer merge together in a wonderfully peaceful way, helping us draw near to God, giving us strength and insight for our daily lives.

Ignatian Prayer: Putting Yourself in a Bible Story

Ignatian prayer is another discipline in which prayer and Bible study merge in a helpful and insightful way. In fact, some might consider Ignatian prayer to be more focused on Bible study than on prayer.

In Ignatian prayer, we place ourselves in a biblical scene and try to become a part of it by using our imagination. We might picture ourselves as one of the main characters in a Bible story, maybe Peter or John in one of the Gospel stories. Or we might imagine ourselves as a bystander in a crowd around Jesus as he heals the leper or talks with the woman who has been bleeding for many years.

Ignatius of Loyola, who lived in the sixteenth century and founded the Jesuit movement, was the great proponent of this method of prayer. It is important to note, however, that this method stands in the long Jewish and Christian tradition of remembering the significance of God's acts in history. The great Jewish holidays—Passover, Hanukkah, Purim, the Festival of Booths—are all firmly rooted in historical events in which God acted. Christmas, Palm Sunday and Easter likewise help us remember what God has done. When we engage in Ignatian prayer, we are remembering and honoring God's acts in history.

Ignatius suggests that as we place ourselves in a biblical story, we try to imagine what we might see, smell, feel and hear, and what the other persons in the scene might be doing. Always, Ignatius says, at each point in this contemplative exercise, we must "try to draw some practical fruit from the reflection for our own life today."[2] We need to ask ourselves what difference it makes in our everyday lives that we

---

Moving Beyond Self-Focus

"*The contemplative experience helped me focus on knowing God and the presence of God and God's love for me. It's what got me outside myself and outside of thinking about how I'm doing in life. The traditions that I grew up with emphasized holiness and obedience. Even though the focus was supposed to be on God, you ended up focusing on yourself and how well you were doing in obeying God. By receiving God's love in contemplative prayer, it freed me from self-focus, and that opened me to other people, to God's work in the world, as well as the character of God in my own life.*"

BEN, *age 56*

---

have encountered God through this Scripture passage. One way to do this is to focus on the words of Jesus and consider the ways our lives would be changed if we heard Jesus say those words to us.

I have returned over and over to the story of the woman at the well in John 4, using Ignatian prayer. I imagine myself as a girl of 8 or 10 playing hide-and-seek with my brother. I'm hiding in the bushes near the well when Jesus comes to talk with the woman. I listen carefully to his words, and as I grow into my teens, his words continue to come back to me. I feel called to grow in worshiping God in spirit and in truth, as Jesus talked about. I am in awe that Jesus knew all about that woman without her telling him, and I ponder what it's like to be known so thoroughly by Jesus. There is something special about that man talking to that woman beside the well, and I ponder in my heart his person and his wisdom.

You can read a passage like the good Samaritan (Lk 10:25-37) and imagine yourself as the person who was attacked, as the person walking by on the other side, and then also as the good Samaritan. As you imagine yourself as each person, what would you feel, see, taste, touch, smell? What would God want to teach you through your connection with each of these characters?

You can imagine yourself as the woman who washes Jesus' feet with her tears (Lk 7:36-50). Why are you weeping? How did you become convinced that Jesus would offer you mercy? Imagine your reaction when you hear him say, "Your sins are forgiven." Perhaps you would like to imagine yourself as one of the other people at the table, watching these events happening.

You can imagine yourself as a shepherd who visits the manger or as a person in the crowd on Palm Sunday or at the crucifixion. All of these exercises help us remember who God is and his faithfulness to us, and bring the truth and reality of God home to our lives today.

Contemplative Prayer and Availability

At its very best, contemplative prayer enables us to abide in Christ. *Abide* means to rest or dwell, and in contemplative prayer we are called to live our lives, more and more each day, in awareness that God is our dwelling place and the place where we rest. In his life on earth, Jesus modeled a radical dependence on God his Father, coupled with a radical availability to people in need. As we grow in our ability to abide in Christ, we will find ourselves drawn into his ministry and his concerns. We cannot love Jesus Christ without loving the people around us.

Richard Foster points out the dangers inherent in the contemplative tradition. He believes that the most common danger is the separation of prayer from everyday life. In addition, he mentions the peril of devaluing intellectual efforts to articulate our faith and the tendency to become so individualistic that we neglect the community of faith.[3]

M. Robert Mulholland Jr., provost of Asbury Theological Seminary, might respond to Richard Foster's concerns in this way: "A life

---

Prayer Is Intimacy with God

"The goal of prayer is prayer, entering into intimacy with God. Period. It's not for the purpose of dealing with midlife or depression or to be better adjusted or anything else. Lectio divina and all those contemplative prayer forms are good, but not if they are confused with prayer itself. Any sorts of patterns will stop working eventually. They can lead you into prayer initially, but they can also get in the way. That's one of the common blinders in the popularizing of spirituality—mistaking the helpful thing for the thing itself. People are self-help junkies, spiritual consumers looking for the next best thing to consume. We are broken people, we need God, and the heart of spirituality is to recognize our brokenness and need for God. We are too quick to replace God with all kinds of tips, ideas, plans, and programs to help us draw near to God."

BRIAN, *age 40*

---

of abiding in God is characterized by a heart whose deepest cry echoes and re-echoes through every aspect of its life—'Thy will be done.'. . . True prayer is a life of radical abiding in God." Later Mulholland writes, "True prayer is a life of radical availability to God in the world."[4]

Surely God's will for me is that I become more like Jesus. This means that I am called to be available to the people God brings into my life, just as Jesus was. The purpose of contemplative prayer is that I would become more and more receptive to God's voice in my life. Therefore, availability is integrally connected to prayer.

If we are available in this way to God, the messages we receive from God will often be practical, even mundane. Joyce Huggett, in *The Joy of Listening to God*, writes, "Early in my prayer pilgrimage, I discovered that listening to God did not necessarily result in mystical experiences. Often, it was not other-worldly at all. Rather, it was a deeply practical affair." She recounts the time she was praying when the words "Ring Valerie" kept coming to her mind. She responded by phoning her friend Valerie at just the right moment to help with a crisis situation.[5]

Over and over as I pray, God has brought to my mind people I need to call, write to or pray for. As I respond in obedience to the voice of God in this way, I continue to grow in my ability to hear his practical instructions to me for how to love the people around me.

Contemplative prayer, at its heart, involves listening to God. This requires time, space and discipline. Ben's story illustrates the benefits of learning to listen for a man who has always had a very active, externally oriented faith.

Ben's Story

Ben is 56 years old, and he works as an administrator at a university. His experience of contemplative prayer has changed the way he meets with God each day in prayer.

*   *   *

In my twenties and thirties, I was a history professor and department chair. I always loved studying and learning and teaching, and I always kept very busy doing it. There simply wasn't a lot of time for reflection. Or, to be more accurate, I didn't choose to take any time for reflection during those years. When I'm honest about it, I can see that in my forties, I didn't have any fewer pressures to do things, it's just that I could no longer resist the pressure from within to spend some amount of time reflecting.

In my forties, I pastored a church and I had to preach every week. Week after week I found myself preaching about the inner journey of faith. What a surprise to me!

I had known about contemplative prayer for years, but I never felt drawn to it until I experienced this irresistible drive to spend time focusing on my inward journey. That's when contemplative prayer began to make sense to me.

Some people call it midlife, but I don't want to trivialize this huge shift that I experienced by giving it such a trite label. To me, it was an earthshaking change, to shift my focus from the outer world of teaching and activities to the inner world of feelings and reflections.

I can see now what a gift it was that I was able to be a pastor when that shift was going on. Each week I had time to study for my sermon. Sure, as a professor I had studied to prepare for my lectures. But that was study of something out there—history. My sermon preparations were truly a study of what was inside, my own personal journey with God.

I began to see the centrality of grace. I had always believed grace was at the heart of the Christian faith, but through contemplative prayer I began to experience God's grace for me. For me! Just for me!

My quiet times changed. Before the shift, I had focused on Bible study and intercessory prayer. Those are both good things, and I still engage in both. After the shift, the center of my quiet time became sitting in silence, waiting for God to speak to me. I've learned that I'm not listening for words or even guidance; I'm looking for an assurance that I am loved. When I take the time in the morning to wait until I have that assurance, my day is transformed. I find I can act out of the abundance of God's grace rather than out of a need to prove myself. This sounds like a small change, but it is a revolutionary difference.

In my fifties, I've returned to a university setting. From the outside, my life looks a lot like it did in my thirties when I chaired the history department at the university where I taught. Every day I'm busy meeting with people, teaching, creating vision, making plans. But now everything is different because I have an attitude of listening to God that permeates everything.

I still try to spend time each morning in the university chapel, waiting until I hear God's word of love and grace for me. All the activities of my days are centered in that voice of love and grace. I'm living my life much more in response to God's initiative now. Before my big shift I lived my life based on what I thought I should be doing.

For me, that's the main point of contemplative prayer: listening to God so our lives can flow out of his love and grace.

* * *

Questions for Reflection

To think about, write about or talk about with friends.

1. Consider the role of silence in your life. What messages did you receive about the significance of silence in your family of origin and in churches you have attended? In what ways did important people in your life value or devalue silence? Do you have fears around being silent?

2. Where are the places in your life where you have experienced silence to be helpful and meaningful? What kinds of circumstances or places help you to be able to engage in reflection? What are the circumstances or places in your life where you have heard God speak to you?

3. Look back over the contemplative prayer disciplines listed in this chapter: breath prayer, *examen*, *lectio divina* and Ignatian prayer.

Does one of them sound attractive to you? Make a plan to experiment with that kind of prayer for a specific period of time, perhaps a week or a month. Write in your calendar a time when you will evaluate what that prayer experience was like for you.

For Further Reading

From the Bible: Psalms 1; 46.

Richard Foster. *Prayer: Finding the Heart's True Home.* New York: HarperSan-Francisco, 1992.

Richard Foster. *Streams of Living Water.* New York: HarperSanFrancisco, 1998.

Richard Foster and James Bryan Smith, eds. *Devotional Classics* (sections 59-143). New York: HarperSanFrancisco, 1993.

Brother Lawrence. *The Practice of the Presence of God.* New Kensington, Penn.: Whitaker House, 1982.

9

Another Look at Midlife

As we come to the last chapter of this book, I want to invite you to consider adopting a new spiritual discipline. Perhaps it will be something described in this book. Perhaps it will be something you have learned about elsewhere. Whatever that new pattern of spirituality is, I am optimistic it will give you hope and freshness as you enter the second half of life.

In addition, I hope that your new spiritual discipline will help you make time for increased reflection and prayer. Bob Buford's very helpful metaphor for midlife, "half time," helps us see clearly that one of the tasks of midlife is to take a break from life in the fast lane in order to reenter the second half of the game with renewed enthusiasm and vision.[1] Most of us really do need some kind of half time at midlife. It may come in the form of a sabbatical with lots of time for reflection. For most of us, though, time for half time reflection will come in snatches, while we are gardening or hiking or attending a contemplative prayer day. We can give ourselves the gift of time for reflection by embracing a new spiritual discipline or pattern of prayer.

Let's listen to Anita, whose midlife reflection has brought about a deep reorientation of her life, integrating her faith and her daily life, her head and her heart, and bringing wholeness and peace in ways she couldn't have imagined.

Anita's Story

Anita, 43, is a nurse who has been a Christian as long as she can remember.

* * *

As we become more mature, we get to know ourselves better. We can no longer hide the truth from ourselves: what we do, what we think. Facing the truth about myself, that's where it all started for me. I have become more true to myself and to God. Therefore, everything else becomes more truthful too.

You grapple with things that haven't come to pass in your life. For me it's love, a mate. It is truly amazing how your heart can deceive you. Our weaknesses sidetrack us—our desire for money, for love. There was one man. I really thought he was the answer for me, and the Lord lets you go your own way when you run after something that hard. God showed me that what I was going after was the wind.

I always thought of myself as a Christian who did the right thing. I identified with the older brother in the parable of the prodigal son in Luke 15. I had to deviate for a while like the younger son. I had to try to get what I wanted on my own, so I could come back home and experience the heart of God, and realize the love and compassion and comfort he offers.

As I looked to God, he showed me myself. He showed me I was

hiding my true, authentic self in order to appeal to men. I had been hitting a lot of dead ends in my life, and the Lord showed me I was going on my own merry way and not looking at him. My life came to a screeching halt.

I sat with the Lord. I began listening to Christian radio on my days off, and God spoke to me through a lot of speakers and preachers. I would sit and read the Word of God. I would pray and fast. The Lord showed me what was really in my heart. He showed me I wasn't speaking my own truth, acknowledging my own true feelings.

I read through the whole Old Testament. I was so struck that all these material things that I wanted—a husband, children, to own my own house—are really second-class things. God showed me he wants us to go first class, and we do that by seeking the things that are above. God spoke to me, saying, "Get your focus off the things of this world, get your focus onto me by surrendering your life, by not being so concerned about what you want."

The Holy Spirit began working in me, convicting me that I needed to tithe, to be generous in giving away 10 percent of my income. For a week it seemed that everything I heard on the radio and everything I read in the Bible was about money. Next came witnessing. I didn't want to witness! The Bible says, "Be anxious for nothing." That's the message when we witness, that God helps us in all situations and gives us peace in all circumstances. For the first time, I felt I actually had something to tell people that could help them. Next came compassion. The Holy Spirit started giving me compassion for people. As God spoke to me about these various issues, I could feel myself relying on the Holy Spirit more each day.

Maybe all this comes from midlife, and your faith goes from your head to your heart because you've tried everything else! We come to the point where we realize we just can't get what we want by our own effort. It's very easy to try to figure out on our own what needs to be done, but what we really need is to seek the heart of God.

My faith used to be dry. Now I feel more whole, more real, more balanced. I've come to realize how easy it is to get the focus off spiritual things because there are so many distractions. In our journey, we need to spend a lot more time with the Lord than we think. Lots of time. Time in quietness.

*   *   *

Anita's time of reflection led her to embrace new spiritual disciplines: tithing, witnessing and showing compassion. Those disciplines then contributed to her continued growth and ability to rely on God. That's the way spiritual disciplines function: as we grow closer to God, we are drawn to increased obedience. Those forms of obedience then help us grow still closer to God.

However, the path is not always smooth, easy and direct! Most people go though periods of feeling distant from God, times of discouragement or hopelessness when God feels far away. The disciplines that used to work so well feel empty and useless. That's when it's helpful to remember the metaphor of life as a journey. Almost all journeys involve places of darkness, uneven paths and steep uphill climbs. At the same time, almost all journeys involve occasional vistas of great beauty.

New spiritual disciplines in our lives can function as fresh paths on the journey, giving us a new direction and a renewed enthusiasm on the road of life. New patterns of prayer and new ways of seeking God can give us the space we need at half time, and they can help us chart a new direction for the second half of life.

Some of the Tasks of Midlife

Nancy Millner, a therapist and coauthor of *Navigating Midlife*, believes that the central task of midlife is to break the tyranny of culture in our lives.[2] She believes that in the first half of life our culture, which includes the influence of our family, exerts an irresistible force. We absorb values and priorities that come from outside ourselves. At midlife we begin the process of shedding the values and priorities of our family and culture, and we begin to find out what is really inside us. We learn the kind of honesty about ourselves that Anita described. We begin to figure out what we really want.

This kind of reflection and reevaluation takes time and space. Many of the spiritual disciplines described in this book give us opportunity for reflection conducted in the presence of God. Many of the people I interviewed about their midlife experiences told me about the joy they have experienced in learning contemplative prayer, which clears the way for time and space in our lives and gives us a structure to hear the voice of God. Sabbath-keeping also creates time which may be used for reflection. Spending time in the out-of-doors and visiting a monastery can also help make the kind of space that is necessary for us to reevaluate our lives and to hear God in the midst of the everyday.

This midlife task of shaking off the culture's values is very real to me right now. Recently I have been hearing the voice of God calling me to reevaluate the way I view my body. I picked up countless messages from the culture and from my family that being thin is good and beautiful and healthy. I hear God telling me it's finally time to break the tyranny of those messages.

I have always been stocky in build. During the decade of the 1980s I battled depression off and on for many years, and I used food for comfort during those painful times. I gained a lot of weight. Since then, I have lost weight a couple of times, but each time I gained it back pretty fast. Now my metabolism has slowed down enough that it is extremely difficult to lose weight—in fact, nearly impossible.

I believe that God loves me just as I am, and I know that many of my friends and colleagues value me just as I am. But there are too many times when I hate myself for being overweight. The pain of being overweight in a culture that values thinness can be overwhelming.

I am beginning to hear God's voice telling me to focus on the positive, not the negative. I am remarkably healthy, and I exercise regularly and enjoy it. Except for pain in my knee, there appear to be no negative health consequences of my weight, and, after all, many thin people have knee trouble. I hear God calling me to be thankful for the body he has given me—something I find very difficult to do.

But even more profoundly, I hear God calling me to shake off our culture's values and live my life for an audience of one: God himself. I never hear a single word from God telling me to lose weight. What I hear from him is that he cares about my heart. He wants my heart to be turned to him, to honor him and love him, to praise him and serve him.

I hear God telling me that fat and thin doesn't matter to him. Often 1 Samuel 16:7 comes into my mind: "The LORD does not see as mortals see: they look on the outward appearance, but the LORD looks on the heart." The people of Israel couldn't see why David was anointed king. His outward appearance was not impressive. They had a preconceived notion of what a king would look like (Saul, their first king, had been strikingly handsome); God wanted a king whose heart was in the right place.

God says to me, *If you have to evaluate your life, there are many "heart" things that are important, and none of them are related to the way your body looks.* Am I honoring the people around me and using my gifts to serve others? Am I drawing near to God in prayer and reading the Bible consistently? Am I trusting God with my deepest longings and desires? And, most significantly, am I going to live my life as if it is God's values that matter, or am I going to continue to beat myself up because my body doesn't measure up to our culture's standards of beauty for a woman?

When Nancy Millner talks about "breaking the tyranny of culture," she is talking about a significant reorientation of thought and values. Many people at midlife are not dealing with their weight in the way that I am, and the factors involved may be different for each of us. But there may be other equally significant cultural values—deeply held ideals that originally came from family, peers, media—that have permeated far into our souls.

A common set of messages that many people received in childhood goes something like this: *Don't express needs, in fact, don't have any needs; be "good" at all times; and for heaven's sake, remember that big boys and big girls don't cry.* Women often heard an additional admonition to meet the needs of people around them at all times without considering their own needs. For men, there were often additional messages related to being a good provider and suppressing all emotions. Continuing to live by these values into the second half of life can be deeply destructive; at midlife many people find they need to discover their own voice and appropriate expression of emotions and needs.

Breaking the tyranny of culture means taking the time to sort through long-held values and decide which ones we want to continue to live by. It means learning to hear God's voice in the midst of the voices from our culture. And it requires receiving help from God in order to know how to move forward.

How can we hear God's voice calling us to freedom and wholeness if we don't take the time to listen? How can we shake off the cultural values that have sunk their roots deep into our very beings without the help of God through his Holy Spirit? How can we discover what's important to us and what we really care about if we don't take time to reflect? We need to find spiritual disciplines that will give us time for reflection and an open heart to hear God's voice. We need patterns of prayer that acknowledge our dependency on the Holy Spirit's work and presence every day and every moment.

Integrating the Neglected Parts

Another way to describe the task of midlife comes from the work of Catherine Fitzgerald, the author of *Developing Leaders*. Fitzgerald is a consultant and executive coach with many midlife clients. She believes that at midlife we begin the process of integrating the neglected, disowned and rejected parts of the self.[3] Anita describes something like this when she says, "We can no longer hide the truth from ourselves: what we do, what we think."

Over the course of our lives, we neglect, disown and reject many different parts of ourselves: things that really should be treated that way, such as our tendency to hatred and violence, and also things that could be positive attributes but that we never felt safe or right about developing. What does it look like to integrate these neglected, disowned and rejected parts of the self?

I can give you one example that seems trivial, but it has been quite significant for me. I was raised by a mother who is very, very tidy. I could never measure up to her level of tidiness, so I stopped trying. I viewed myself as an untidy slob for most of my life, and I did very little to cultivate any habits of tidiness. I completely neglected, disowned and rejected any fragment of tidiness I might have had.

A few years ago I dug out a box of dolls from my childhood. In the box were two Barbie dolls with a tangle of clothes, shoes, purses and other small items. I took all of it to a doll dealer. She showed me the original booklets from the 1960s that had come with the dolls. The booklets had pictures of each clothing outfit with all the accessories that had come in the original package with the outfit.

The doll dealer and I sorted through all the clothes and miscellaneous items and arranged everything to match the outfits in the catalog. To my surprise, not one tiny earring or shoe or purse was missing. Each outfit I had saved for so many years was complete with all its parts.

I realized that I couldn't have been a totally untidy child. No ten-year-old could have played with Barbie dolls hour after hour without losing a single tiny item unless that child was a fairly tidy individual. In fact, I realized I am innately a moderately tidy person, but in the face of my mother's extreme tidiness, I never made any effort to develop that attribute. In fact, I shoved it aside for more than forty years.

In the past few years, I have experimented with tidiness, and I find I like it! I like the peacefulness of tidy spaces. In the frenzy of everyday life, some degree of order is restful and calming, and I need every bit of rest and calm that I can find. I am reclaiming a part of myself that was totally cut off. I'm the one who cut it off, and I'm the one who is reclaiming it, with God's help. I'm discovering a new value that comes from a hidden place inside.

I am finding I have to be very patient with myself as I reclaim this rejected part of myself. It takes time to acquire new skills. I am learning the skills of tidiness that I could have been learning over a lifetime, but didn't. And I'm being careful not to set unrealistically high goals—*moderate* neatness is what I'm aiming for.

People have told me about many other positive things that they have found buried in themselves. One woman always believed she was incompetent in math. At 50, she was stunned to find herself excelling in an accounting class required for her job. Her success in the class caused a lot of soul searching as she pondered how and why she had come to believe she couldn't do well at math.

Many people, both men and women, find they need to reclaim their passionate selves. In the face of all those childhood messages to be "good" all the time, never to cry, never to have emotional needs, many of us disowned and rejected the ability to experience and express any sort of passions. What does it look like to get angry appropriately? Will I ever be able to get tears in my eyes in public settings without being paralyzed with embarrassment? What do my tears mean? When I really care about things, how can I learn to feel comfortable expressing my concern with energy and enthusiasm? These are some of the questions that require time for reflection and prayer.

Finding these constructive things inside and learning to nurture them is a challenge. But even more challenging is the reality that there are also many negative things buried deep inside us—the impulse to kill people when we are angry, the desire to have sex with a stranger on the street, the longing to have the world center around us with everything going our way. At midlife, despite our best intentions to keep these undesirable parts of ourselves hidden, some of them may emerge into our conscious thoughts, and we'll be shocked at what we find.

If we have established healthy and comfortable patterns of prayer and reflection, we will have greater ability to cope with these disturbing thoughts when they surface. It takes time, attention and prayer to grow in coping with the negative parts of ourselves that we have spent twenty some years ignoring, pretending they don't exist. To integrate these negative parts of ourselves, we will have to grow in honesty in our prayers of confession. We will also have to do some deep reflection about how we want to respond to the reality that we aren't quite as pure and innocent as we like to pretend we are. Negative parts of ourselves are real, and our task is to honestly accept those parts, integrate them into the way we view ourselves and learn how to respond appropriately to them in our daily lives.

Several of the disciplines described in this book will be helpful in the task of integrating these positive and negative parts of ourselves. Any discipline that provides time for reflection will probably be helpful. Praying the Psalms has been very helpful to me in honestly acknowledging the negative emotions and desires inside me. The Celtic Christian tradition with all its beautiful poetry can also help us with the task of integration. Celtic poetry and prayer present such a holistic and unified view of reality; we are encouraged to bring every aspect of our lives to God. Through Celtic Christianity we experience the reality that there is nothing hidden from God, nothing is outside the bounds of God's forgiving, healing and restoring love, and there is nothing in our lives that cannot reflect God's glory and presence.

The practice of "soul nurture" can also help us with the task of integration of all the parts of ourselves. As we bring our hearts to God and experience a heartfelt connection with God, we grow in experiencing the reality that God accepts us just as we are. There is no part of our inner selves that cannot be brought into the light. Past hurts, unfulfilled dreams, long-held grudges, petty irritations and unkind judgments are a part of us. God longs for us to face these less-than-attractive aspects of our inner being. He longs to forgive us, heal us and give us a fresh start. He can use even those parts of our lives for good (Rom 8:28), but he can't do that until we acknowledge they are there.

Mystery and Community

Two additional tasks of midlife particularly affect baby boomers and some older Gen-X folks. We were raised in a time, the 1950s and 1960s, that emphasized human autonomy and scientific truth more than any other era before or since. Part of what we have to do at midlife is develop an understanding of our place in community, as well as a view of truth that includes a place for mystery.

The way schools now teach science captures some of these changes in thought. Most of us studied frogs by dissecting them; now high school science classes are more likely to study frogs as a part of the ecosystem where they live. In our school years, plants and animals were studied as if they existed independently of everything around them, reinforcing society's passion for individuality and objectivity. In science classes now there is much more emphasis now on the web of life and the interconnectedness of all living beings.

Many people have talked with me about their growing understanding during their midlife years of their interconnectedness with the people around them. At midlife we learn more of what it means to be truly ourselves while also a being part of a web of relationships. We learn what interdependence will look like for us and how we can embrace it.

We grow in understanding the place of both dependence and independence in a healthy life. Our culture values independence so highly that we easily forget that we are called to both giving and receiving. Kathleen Fischer, a therapist and spiritual director, writes in her book *Winter Grace*, "The Christian vision is of an *interdependent* community of persons who are all both weak and strong in various ways and who mutually exchange their gifts."[4]

Fischer goes on to say:

> Dependence is an intrinsic dimension of all existence. Interdependence is a fact of life and does not decrease personal worth. We begin our life as a gift from others, and The Other, God. Life is lived in communion from the beginning. Our existence is always partly a gift from others; we feed upon one another. Farmers produce the food we eat; artists, writers and philosophers contribute to the growth of our minds and spirits. We turn to friends for courage and support; all those people we come into contact with enter in some way into the fabric of our being. Maturity is not defined exclusively in terms of independence; rather, it is the ability both to give and to receive, to influence and be influenced.[5]

At midlife, as you try out new patterns of spirituality, look for the ways God may be affirming your call to community, to places and relationships where you can both give and receive. As we separate from our parents' values and other cultural values we have absorbed, we become more clear about who we are. But at the same time, we are more aware of the ways we need people around us, of the ways we influence others and allow ourselves to be influenced. We may find ourselves reevaluating our friendships or lack of relationships. We may choose not to nurture old friendships that are getting in the way of the growth we are moving toward, and we may seek out new friends with whom we can walk in new paths.

At midlife most of us grow in accepting the reality of a journey inward; we are called now to tend the roots of the tree that is our life, after decades of growing externally visible branches and fruit. However, this journey inward is most healthy if it is experienced in community with others who are on the same journey. In what ways is God calling you to walk with others, to give and receive? Who are the people God has placed beside you on your journey, and in what ways do you allow yourself to depend on them? In what ways do you allow them to depend on you? In what ways do you influence others and allow others to influence you?

This growth in interdependence flies in the face of the culture of our childhood and young adult years, which emphasized independence and autonomy. In addition, at midlife we will probably need to address another one of our culture's influences: the emphasis on objective truth. Again, we can see a shift in this area by observing the way science is taught. In science classrooms today, truth has a component of mystery that was lacking in the 1950s and 1960s.

Here's one example. Light behaves like a particle when viewed with one set of assumptions, and it behaves like a wave when observed from another viewpoint. What is true about light? Is it a wave or a particle? It can't be both! Yet somehow both are true at the same time, and there is no way the two views can be totally reconciled.

As our culture shifts from an objective view of truth to a view of truth more accepting of mystery, we midlife baby boomers and almost-midlife Gen-Xers will probably find ourselves changing the way we view truth, at least to some extent. I have said elsewhere in this book that at midlife I have become more certain of key issues— God's grace at the root of everything, God's love in Jesus Christ, God's call to love him and serve him—at the same time that I have become less certain about some other peripheral questions. What issues are central for you? What truth are you willing to die for? What do you continue to affirm to be true even as you learn to embrace mystery?

I experience a sense of joy and peace in my growing certainty that there is much about God that I cannot understand. God dwells in unimaginable majesty and glory, and I can only get glimpses of his reality. God works in our world in ways that are beyond my comprehension. I simply cannot know or explain everything. God has given us enough knowledge of his character and love for us to draw near to him, but he has not revealed everything to us. Learning to rest in that sense of mystery has been a peaceful part of my midlife journey.

The spiritual disciplines described in this book will be helpful as you sort out issues of individuality, community and interdependence

---

Mystery

In understanding and articulating the Christian faith, we must make room for the concept of "mystery"—not as an irrational complement to the rational but as a reminder that the fundamental reality of God transcends human rationality.
STANLEY GRENZ, *A Primer on Postmodernism*

---

and as you consider the place of truth and mystery in your life of faith. It takes time and silence to consider these questions, to allow ourselves to hear God's voice and our own inner voice. All of the disciplines described in this book help provide structure for individual reflection and listening. They are also rich and full if exercised in community.

I hope and pray that you will find fresh paths that will enable you to accomplish the tasks of midlife described here: to shake off the values you got from your culture and find your own, to grow in accepting the disowned and rejected parts of yourself, and to embrace interdependence and mystery in ways that are life-giving for you.

My Prayer for You

In this book, we have looked at the losses and discoveries of midlife, and we have looked at a handful of spiritual disciplines that can be helpful at midlife. We have considered some of the developmental tasks of midlife. As you navigate your midlife journey, I wish you joy and discovery and freshness. I hope and pray that through this book you may find a new or renewed spiritual path to help you make the transition to the second half of life.

We are not alone in the midlife journey. Many others have gone before us and walk alongside us. I hope and pray that you will find comforting and challenging friends for the journey, and that some of the voices you have heard in this book will be companions for you.

God goes with us as well. God's Holy Spirit is in us, whispering words of comfort and direction and enabling us to walk in right paths. Jesus, the "man of sorrows, acquainted with grief" (Is 53:3), walks beside us. There is no part of our inner being that Jesus cannot understand. There is no grief, no disappointment, no accumulation of losses that he cannot sympathize with. If the losses of midlife pile up for you, I pray that you will be drawn to depend on Christ in new ways, and that you will experience his nearness and comfort in your sorrow. As you make the discoveries that so often come at midlife, I am hopeful that you will have the strong sense of God's guidance into those discoveries, God's partnership with you as you grow, and a sense of God's delight in you as a person in the wonderful—and challenging—midlife years.

Notes

Preface

[1]Bob Buford, *Half Time: Changing Your Game Plan from Success to Significance* (Grand Rapids, Mich.: Zondervan, 1994).

Acknowledgments

[1]Lynne M. Baab, *Embracing Midlife: Congregations as Support Systems* (Washington D.C.: The Alban Institute, 1999).

Chapter 1: The Losses of Midlife

[1]James Harnish, *Men at Midlife: Steering Through the Detours* (Nashville: Dimensions for Living, 1993).

Chapter 3: Finding God in All of Life: Celtic Christian Spirituality

[1]Esther de Waal, *The Celtic Way of Prayer* (New York: Doubleday, 1997), p. 27.

[2]Alexander Carmichael, ed., *Carmina Gadelica I* (Scottish Academic Press, 1900), p. 3.

[3]Bruce Reed Pullen, *Discovering Celtic Christianity* (Mystic, Conn.: Twenty-Third Publications, 1999), pp. 10-12.

[4]De Waal, *Celtic Way of Prayer*, pp. 2-3.

[5]Sr. John Miriam Jones, S.C., *With an Eagle's Eye* (Notre Dame, Ind.: Ave Maria Press, 1998), p. 65.

[6]De Waal, *Celtic Way of Prayer*, pp. 36-37.

[7]Ibid., pp. 38-39.

[8]Eleanor Hull, *The Poem Book of the Gael*, quoted in de Waal, *Celtic Way of Prayer*, pp. 39-40.

[9]Douglas Hyde, *Religious Songs of Connacht, Volume II* (London: Dublin, 1906; reprint, Irish University Press, 1972), p. 39.

[10]Pullen, *Discovering Celtic Christianity*, pp. 72-79, 122-30.

[11]Jones, *With an Eagle's Eye*, p. 28.

[12]Ibid., pp. 58-59.

[13]Carmichael, *Carmina Gadelica II*, quoted in de Waal, *Celtic Way of Prayer*, pp. 203-4.

[14]G. Murphy, *Early Irish Lyrics* (Oxford, England: Oxford University Press, 1956), p. 4.

[15]Quoted in de Waal, *Celtic Way of Prayer*, p. 188.

[16]Carmichael, *Carmina Gadelica II*, pp. 54-61, quoted in de Waal, *Celtic Way of Prayer*, p. 205.

[17]De Waal, *Celtic Way of Prayer*, p. 123.

Chapter 4: Enjoying God's World: Worshiping the Creator

[1]Gordon MacDonald, "Foreword," in *The Best Preaching on Earth: Sermons on Caring for Creation*, ed. Stan L. LeQuire (Valley Forge, Penn.: Judson Press, 1996), p. xvi.

[2]John R. W. Stott, "The Works of the Lord," in *Best Preaching on Earth*, p. 82.

[3]Ron Sider, "Tending the Garden Without Worshipping It," in *Best Preaching on Earth*, p. 37.

[4]Calvin DeWitt, "Creation's Care and Keeping," in *Simpler Living, Compassionate Life*, ed. Michael Schut (Denver, Colo.: Living the Good News, 1999), p. 176.

[5]Howard Snyder, "This World is Not My Home?" in *Best Preaching on Earth*, p. 46.

[6]Richard Foster, "The Discipline of Simplicity," in *Simpler Living, Compassionate Life*, p. 182.

[7]Cecile Andrews, "The Spirituality of Everyday Life," in *Simpler Living, Compassionate Life*, pp. 38-39.

Chapter 5: Resting in God: Sabbath-Keeping

[1]C. S. Lewis, *Perelandra* (New York: Macmillan, 1944), p. 217.

[2]Dorothy C. Bass, "Keeping Sabbath: Reviving a Christian Practice," *Christian Century*, January 1-8, 1997, p. 15.

[3]Abraham Joshua Heschel, *The Sabbath* (New York: Farrar, Straus & Giroux, 1951, 1979), p. 13.

[4]Bonnie Thurston, *To Everything a Season: A Spirituality of Time* (New York: Crossroad, 1999), pp. 29, 47.

[5]Heschel, *Sabbath*, p. 74.

[6]Tilden Edwards, *Sabbath Time* (Nashville: Upper Room, 1992), p. 134.

[7]Wayne Muller, *Sabbath: Restoring the Sacred Rhythm of Rest* (New York: Bantam, 1999), p. 27.

[8]Edwards, *Sabbath Time*, p. 90.

Chapter 6: Embracing Discipline: Benedictine Spirituality

[1]Paul Wilkes, *Beyond the Walls: Monastic Wisdom for Everyday Life* (New York: Doubleday, 1999), pp. 4-5.

[2]Ibid., p. 10.

[3]Ibid., p. 68.

[4]Ibid., p. 69.

[5]Timothy Fry, OSB, ed., *The Rule of St. Benedict in English* (Collegeville, Minn.: The Liturgical Press, 1981), prologue 35.

[6]Elizabeth Canham, *Heart Whispers: Benedictine Wisdom for Today* (Nashville: Upper Room, 1999), p. 110.

[7]Ibid., p. 111.

[8]Wilkes, *Beyond the Walls*, pp. 45-46.

[9]Esther de Waal, *Living with Contradiction: An Introduction to Benedictine Spirituality* (Harrisburg, Penn.: Morehouse, 1989, 1997), p. 30.

[10]Ibid., p. 52.

[11]Canham, *Heart Whispers*, pp. 140-41.

[12]Ibid., p. 140.

[13]De Waal, *Living with Contradiction*, pp. 53-54.

[14]Kathleen Norris, *The Cloister Walk* (New York: Riverhead, 1996), p. xiii.

Chapter 7: Soul Nurture: Drawing Near to God with the Heart

[1]Thomas Moore, *Care of the Soul* (New York: HarperCollins, 1992), pp. xi-xii.

[2]Brent Curtis and John Eldredge, *The Sacred Romance: Drawing Closer to the Heart of God* (Nashville: Thomas Nelson, 1997), p. 3.

[3]Ibid., p. 6.

[4]Ibid.

[5]Ibid., p. 179.

[6]Gerald May, "Entering the Emptiness," in *Simpler Living, Compassionate Life*, ed. Michael Schut (Denver, Colo: Living the Good News, 1999), p. 48.

[7]Ibid.

[8]C. S. Lewis, *The Weight of Glory and Other Addresses* (New York: Macmillan, 1980), p. 16.

[9]J. R. R. Tolkien, "On Fairy-Stories," in *Essays Presented to Charles Williams*, ed. C. S. Lewis (Grand Rapids, Mich.: Eerdmans, 1981), p. 81.

[10]Lewis, *The Weight of Glory*, pp. 16-17.

[11]David Rensberger, "Thirsty for God," *Weavings*, July/August 2000, p. 23.

[12]Ibid., p. 25.

Chapter 8: Listening to God: The Contemplative Christian Tradition

[1]Richard Foster, *Streams of Living Water* (San Francisco: HarperSanFrancisco, 1998), pp. 32-33.

[2]Chester P. Michael and Marie C. Norrisey, *Prayer and Temperament* (Charlottesville, Va.: The Open Door, 1984), p. 53.

[3]Foster, *Streams of Living Water*, pp. 53-56.

[4]M. Robert Mulholland Jr., "Prayer as Availability to God," *Weavings*, September/October 1997, pp. 24-25.

[5]Joyce Huggett, *The Joy of Listening to God* (Downers Grove, Ill.: InterVarsity Press, 1986), pp. 205-6.

Chapter 9: Another Look at Midlife

[1]Bob Buford, *Half Time: Changing Your Game Plan from Success to Significance* (Grand Rapids, Mich.: Zondervan, 1994).

[2]Nancy Millner, in an address at the International Conference of the Association for Psychological Type, Minneapolis, June 2001. She is coauthor of *Navigating Midlife: Using Typology as a Guide* (Palo Alto, Calif.: Consulting Psychologists Press, 1993).

[3]Catherine Fitzgerald, in an address at the International Conference of the Association for Psychological Type, Minneapolis, June 2001. She is coauthor of *Developing Leaders: Research and Applications in Psychological Type* (Palo Alto, Calif.: Davies Black Publishing, 1997).

[4]Kathleen Fischer, *Winter Grace: Spirituality and Aging* (Nashville: Upper Room, 1998), p. 67.

[5]Ibid., p. 69.